Supercharge Your JavaScript

Using AI for Smarter, Faster Development

By Laurence Lars Svekis

Dedicated to

Alexis and Sebastian

Thank you for your support

For more content and to learn more, visit
https://basescripts.com

Introduction

Welcome! If you're reading this book, chances are you're curious about JavaScript and how AI can help you learn it more easily, use it more effectively, and build real things faster than ever before. You might be completely new to coding or someone who's tried a few tutorials but got stuck somewhere between theory and actually building something. Wherever you are on your journey, this book was made for you.

In this chapter, we'll explore how AI is reshaping the way we approach JavaScript development—and how adopting the right mindset can transform you from a "do-it-all" beginner into a confident, creative problem solver. Let's start by looking at how AI changes everything.

Learning Objectives

By the end of this chapter, you will:

- Understand how AI changes the way developers work and learn.

- Identify how AI can reduce the burden of manual coding and debugging.

- Begin developing the mindset of a "developer as architect" rather than a "developer as builder."

- Set expectations for what this book will help you do—with the help of AI.

- Feel motivated and equipped to dive into JavaScript with confidence.

Why AI Is a Game-Changer for Developers

Traditionally, learning to code meant years of trial-and-error. Beginners had to memorize syntax, troubleshoot cryptic errors, and figure out how to "build something real" without knowing where to start. Many gave up before reaching the fun parts.

Now, with AI, you're never alone when learning to code. You can:

- Ask questions in plain language and get immediate, helpful answers.

- Generate working JavaScript examples based on simple prompts.

- Debug broken code by showing it to AI and asking, "What's wrong here?"

- Explore multiple solutions and choose the one that fits your style or goals.

AI doesn't do the thinking for you — it gives you the space to think more clearly.

Real-World Example

Let's say you want to build a simple calculator but don't know where to start.

Prompt to AI:

> "Create a simple JavaScript calculator with add, subtract, multiply, and divide functions. Make it usable in the browser with buttons."

Within seconds, AI can give you a full HTML/JS layout, complete with event listeners and basic styling. Suddenly, you're working with something real — and improving it, tweaking it, understanding it.

Moving from "Doing It All" to "Guiding Smarter Work"

In the past, developers had to handle every small detail: typing every bracket, solving every bug, and remembering every function by heart. With AI, the role shifts.

Instead of being a laborer writing every line of code, you become a **guide**, directing the work, checking for quality, and refining ideas.

Here's what that shift looks like:

Traditional Developer Role	AI-Powered Developer Role
Write everything from scratch	Prompt for code and edit
Memorize every method	Ask AI for quick lookups
Get stuck on bugs for hours	Use AI to identify and fix bugs
Learn alone through trial	Collaborate with AI in real time

This shift frees you to focus on creativity, structure, design, and user experience — all the things that make software exciting and impactful.

Mindset Shift: Developer as Architect, Not Just Builder

Builders follow blueprints. Architects design them.

In the world of AI-assisted development, you are becoming the **architect** of your projects. Instead of focusing only on syntax, you'll learn to think about:

- **What should this code do?**

- **How will people use it?**

- **How can it be made simpler or better?**

- **What's the best way to organize or reuse this logic?**

By prompting AI carefully, evaluating the results critically, and improving based on what you learn, you're no longer just coding — you're designing, directing, and innovating.

Example: From Prompt to Product

You might ask AI:

> "Build a JavaScript function that creates a pop-up form for newsletter signup and saves the email in localStorage."

AI gives you a solid starting point. But as the architect, you might:

- Change the styling to match your site.

- Add validation to the form.

- Store data in a more secure or scalable way later.

The AI builds the first version. You bring the vision to life.

What This Book Will Help You Achieve

This book is not about becoming an expert in JavaScript syntax overnight. It's about helping you:

- **Start building real things—fast**
  Even with zero coding experience, you'll learn how to describe what you want and let AI help you make it happen.

- **Learn by doing, not just watching**
  You'll interact with code, tweak it, break it, fix it, and understand it—using AI as your learning assistant.

- **Overcome the "blank page" problem**
  You'll never be stuck wondering *where* to start. AI can provide the skeleton, and you fill in the heart.

- **Build confidence as a developer**
  By the end of this book, you'll feel comfortable prompting AI to assist you with anything from small scripts to full-featured apps.

- **Take ownership of your learning**
  Instead of following rigid tutorials, you'll learn to explore, experiment, and solve problems your own way—with AI by your side.

Action Items for This Chapter

Before diving into the next chapter, complete these action steps to get the most out of this book:

1. **Reflect:**
   Think about one JavaScript project you've always wanted to build. Write it down in plain English.

2. **Prompt Practice:**
   Open your preferred AI tool (e.g., ChatGPT, Gemini, Claude, or Codeium) and try a basic prompt like:
   "Create a JavaScript function that adds two numbers and returns the result."

3. **Mindset Shift:**
   Write down three sentences starting with:

   - *I used to think coding was...*

   - *Now I think coding with AI is...*

   - *This book will help me...*

4. **Create a Workspace:**
   Set up a folder on your computer or in the cloud (like Google Drive) to store your projects, snippets, and notes as you go through this book.

5. **Start Exploring:**
   Ask AI a question you've always wanted to understand about JavaScript — like "What is a closure?" or "Why use arrow functions?"

You're not just about to learn JavaScript.

You're about to learn how to *think like a developer*, write code with confidence, and explore a whole new way of building through collaboration with AI.

Chapter 1: Rethinking Your Workflow with AI

A Beginner's Guide to JavaScript - Using AI to Learn and Code Smarter

Learning Objectives

By the end of this chapter, you'll be able to:

- Clearly understand what JavaScript coding tasks AI can (and can't) handle.

- Use AI to streamline your workflow, save time, and maintain high code quality.

- Focus on higher-level tasks like design and architecture.

- Confidently use AI to practically develop and debug JavaScript through examples and exercises.

Introduction to AI-Assisted JavaScript

Artificial Intelligence (AI) has revolutionized how beginners approach coding. Rather than spending countless hours learning syntax and debugging manually, you can leverage AI tools to quickly write and improve your JavaScript. This chapter will guide you through effectively using AI to make JavaScript development easier, faster, and more enjoyable.

What Tasks AI Can (and Can't) Handle

✅ **Tasks AI Can Handle:**

- **Generating code snippets** from simple descriptions.

- **Debugging** JavaScript errors.

- **Explaining** JavaScript code clearly.

- **Refactoring** code for improved readability and performance.

Example:

Prompt: *"Create a JavaScript function that checks if a number is even."*

AI-generated Code:

```
function isEven(num) {

    return num % 2 === 0;

}
```

Practice Exercise:

Prompt AI: *"Explain step-by-step how the above function works."*
Review the detailed explanation provided.

⊘ Tasks AI Cannot Handle:

- Fully understanding vague instructions.

- Completely replacing human creativity.

- Predicting complex context without clear instructions.

Saving Time Without Sacrificing Quality

AI significantly reduces repetitive coding work, freeing up your time to think creatively and strategically.

Traditional vs. AI-enhanced Examples:

Task	Traditional Approach	AI-enhanced Approach
Writing loops	Manually coding each loop	Quick prompt-based generation
Form validation	Researching methods extensively	AI-generated ready-to-use code
Debugging common errors	Searching forums extensively	Immediate AI-driven solutions

Action Item:

Use an AI tool to quickly generate JavaScript code for formatting the current date as "MM/DD/YYYY".

Focusing on Higher-Level Design and Architecture

AI enables you to shift your focus to the bigger picture — defining what your application should do and how it should interact with users.

Checklist for High-Level Thinking:

- Define clear project goals and user interactions.

- Break down complex tasks into simpler functions.

- Clearly communicate your needs to the AI assistant.

Exercise:

Describe a basic application idea (e.g., task manager), and ask AI to outline JavaScript functions required to create it.

Practical Examples & Exercises

Example 1: Calculator Function

Prompt: *"Create a JavaScript function that calculates addition, subtraction, multiplication, and division."*

AI-generated Code:

```
function calculate(a, b) {

  return {

    add: a + b,

    subtract: a - b,

    multiply: a * b,

    divide: b !== 0 ? a / b : 'Cannot divide
by zero'

  };

}
```

Exercise 1:

Test the calculator function by creating a basic HTML page that interacts with user inputs.

Example 2: Debugging with AI

Faulty Code Provided:

```javascript
let age = prompt("Enter your age");

if(age = 18){

  console.log("You are 18!");

}
```

Prompt to AI: *"Fix the JavaScript code above."*

AI Correction:

```javascript
let age = prompt("Enter your age");

if(age == 18){

  console.log("You are 18!");

}
```

Exercise 2:

Implement and test the corrected code.

Comprehensive Quiz: 25 Multiple-Choice Questions with Answers and Explanations

Question 1: What JavaScript task is AI particularly good at handling?
A. Emotional decision-making
B. Writing code snippets
C. Artistic creation
D. Planning vacations
Answer: B
Explanation: AI excels at quickly writing JavaScript code snippets based on descriptions.

Question 2: A major limitation of AI-generated code is:
A. It never makes mistakes
B. It can misunderstand vague instructions
C. It replaces creativity completely
D. It always predicts context correctly
Answer: B
Explanation: AI needs clear instructions; vague prompts can lead to misunderstanding.

Question 3: How does AI primarily save developers' time?
A. By eliminating testing
B. By handling repetitive coding tasks
C. By automatically publishing websites
D. By physically building computers
Answer: B
Explanation: AI quickly manages routine coding tasks, significantly saving time.

Question 4: What should you always do after receiving AI-generated code?
A. Immediately deploy it
B. Test and review thoroughly
C. Assume it's always correct
D. Rewrite from scratch
Answer: B
Explanation: AI-generated code always requires testing and verification.

Question 5: Refactoring refers to:
A. Deleting unnecessary code
B. Writing entirely new features
C. Improving existing code without changing functionality
D. Compiling code
Answer: C
Explanation: Refactoring improves code structure and readability without altering functionality.

Question 6: AI struggles most with:
A. Simple, clear tasks
B. Ambiguous instructions
C. Detailed prompts
D. Structured requests
Answer: B
Explanation: AI tools find vague, ambiguous instructions difficult to interpret correctly.

Question 7: Effective AI prompts should be:
A. Random
B. Clear and concise
C. Lengthy
D. Vague
Answer: B
Explanation: Clear and concise prompts yield the most accurate AI-generated results.

Question 8: What task is beyond AI's capability currently?
A. Code debugging
B. Understanding implicit context without explanation
C. Generating JavaScript functions
D. Explaining code snippets
Answer: B
Explanation: AI cannot reliably infer implicit context without explicit details.

Question 9: The key to successfully using AI in coding is:
 A. Trusting it completely
 B. Providing detailed prompts and verifying outcomes
 C. Avoiding human interaction
 D. Minimizing its use
Answer: B
Explanation: Precise prompts and thorough review ensure AI-generated code quality.

Question 10: AI assists non-coders most effectively by:
 A. Writing legal documents
 B. Cooking meals
 C. Handling basic coding tasks
 D. Doing physical hardware repairs
Answer: C
Explanation: AI simplifies basic coding tasks, making programming more accessible for non-coders.

Question 11: AI-generated JavaScript is most useful for:
 A. Building entire applications independently
 B. Writing repetitive scripts
 C. Physical labor tasks
 D. Creating financial audits
Answer: B
Explanation: AI is particularly effective for generating repetitive coding scripts.

Question 12: AI-generated code quality heavily depends on:
 A. Emotional intelligence of the AI
 B. Quality and clarity of the prompt
 C. Physical environment
 D. The price of AI software
Answer: B
Explanation: Prompt clarity directly influences the quality of AI-generated outputs.

Question 13: Can AI replace human coders completely?
A. Yes, immediately
B. Only in art projects
C. No, it complements human coding skills
D. Yes, but only temporarily
Answer: C
Explanation: AI complements rather than replaces human coding capabilities.

Question 14: Debugging effectively with AI involves:
A. Using vague descriptions
B. Providing exact error messages
C. Ignoring AI suggestions
D. Avoiding interactions with AI
Answer: B
Explanation: Exact error messages enable AI to quickly identify and suggest solutions.

Question 15: Using AI-generated code safely involves:
A. Immediate deployment
B. Thorough testing and reviewing
C. Avoiding testing completely
D. Trusting AI implicitly
Answer: B
Explanation: Always thoroughly test AI-generated code before deploying.

Question 16: AI assists in JavaScript learning primarily by:
A. Completely replacing practice
B. Automatically passing coding exams
C. Clarifying complex coding concepts
D. Removing any need for coding knowledge
Answer: C
Explanation: AI clearly explains complex coding concepts, helping learners understand JavaScript better.

Question 17: Refactoring JavaScript code with AI means:
A. Writing completely new code
B. Optimizing existing code structure
C. Deleting code unnecessarily
D. Uploading code online
Answer: B
Explanation: Refactoring is optimizing existing code for better readability and performance.

Question 18: To ensure the accuracy of AI-generated JavaScript, developers must:
A. Trust implicitly without verification
B. Cross-check results through testing
C. Avoid using AI entirely
D. Use AI-generated code immediately
Answer: B
Explanation: Always cross-check AI-generated code through careful testing.

Question 19: AI coding tools help beginners by:
A. Performing physical installations
B. Replacing all coding knowledge
C. Simplifying learning through clear examples
D. Completely automating coding projects
Answer: C
Explanation: AI tools provide practical examples, significantly aiding beginner learning.

Question 20: Optimal AI prompts are:
A. Short and unclear
B. Clear and goal-oriented
C. Lengthy and confusing
D. Randomly generated
Answer: B
Explanation: Clear, goal-oriented prompts yield accurate AI outputs.

Question 21: Which coding aspect does AI significantly enhance?
 A. Creativity entirely
 B. Repetitive tasks and debugging
 C. Physical hardware setup
 D. Financial planning
 Answer: B
 Explanation: AI significantly streamlines repetitive coding tasks and debugging processes.

Question 22: AI tools generally perform poorly with:
 A. Clear instructions
 B. Ambiguous or unclear requests
 C. Structured tasks
 D. Technical coding prompts
 Answer: B
 Explanation: AI struggles with ambiguous requests due to difficulty interpreting context.

Question 23: AI's primary role in coding is to:
 A. Replace humans entirely
 B. Support and enhance human tasks
 C. Manage employees directly
 D. Write novels
 Answer: B
 Explanation: AI primarily supports and enhances human coding tasks.

Question 24: Effective debugging with AI means:
 A. Ignoring AI outputs
 B. Providing vague descriptions
 C. Copying exact error messages to AI
 D. Avoiding interaction
 Answer: C
 Explanation: Exact errors provided to AI tools result in precise debugging suggestions.

Question 25: The most crucial factor for effective AI-assisted coding is:

A. Avoiding AI use

B. Trusting AI blindly

C. Precise prompts and careful review of AI outputs

D. Minimal human oversight

Answer: C

Explanation: Success with AI-assisted coding depends on clear prompts and thorough review.

Chapter 2: Setting Up Your AI Toolkit

Welcome to your practical guide for getting set up with the best AI tools to accelerate your JavaScript development journey, even as a complete beginner!

Learning Objectives:

By the end of this chapter, you'll be able to:

- Identify the best AI tools available for JavaScript development.

- Understand each tool's strengths and ideal use cases.

- Select the appropriate AI tool based on your specific coding task.

- Integrate AI tools seamlessly into your existing development environment.

- Confidently start using AI for practical JavaScript development tasks.

Best AI Tools for JavaScript Developers

AI tools have become indispensable partners for beginners learning JavaScript. Here are some leading AI coding assistants you should know:

1. ChatGPT (OpenAI)

- **Strengths:** Versatile, conversational coding assistant. Great at explaining concepts, generating code snippets, debugging, and learning support.

- **Ideal for:** Beginners seeking clear explanations and step-by-step guidance.

Example use:
Prompt: *"Explain what a JavaScript array is and how to use it."* ChatGPT will provide a detailed, beginner-friendly explanation with examples.

2. GitHub Copilot (GitHub/Microsoft)

- **Strengths:** Real-time code suggestions directly in your code editor. Excellent for writing repetitive code or boilerplate quickly.

- **Ideal for:** Quickly writing JavaScript functions, loops, or repetitive logic.

Example use:
You type:

```
function greet(name) {
```

GitHub Copilot automatically suggests completing it:

```
  return `Hello, ${name}!`;

}
```

3. Claude (Anthropic)

- **Strengths:** Clear, detailed explanations and robust coding examples. Focused on accuracy and safe AI coding.

- **Ideal for:** High-quality explanations and detailed, error-free code generation.

4. Codeium

- **Strengths:** Fast, accurate code completion with minimal lag. Excellent for fast-paced coding tasks and real-time assistance.

- **Ideal for:** Rapid development and high productivity during active coding sessions.

Choosing the Right AI for the Right Task

Not every AI tool excels at every task. Matching your task to the AI's strengths is key to efficiency and accuracy.

Quick Selection Checklist:

- **Code generation & repetitive tasks:** GitHub Copilot, Codeium

- **Clear explanations & detailed examples:** ChatGPT, Claude

- **Debugging & troubleshooting:** ChatGPT, Claude

- **Fast, real-time coding suggestions:** Codeium, GitHub Copilot

Exercise: Pick Your AI Assistant

Scenario: You want detailed explanations of JavaScript concepts.
 Action:

- Which tool should you choose? *(Answer: ChatGPT or Claude)*

- Prompt it: *"What is a JavaScript function, and give me two examples."*

Integrating AI into Your Existing Dev Stack

Integrating AI seamlessly means setting up your development environment to easily use these tools directly where you write code.

Step-by-Step Integration:

Step 1: Install Code Editor (e.g., VS Code)
 Download and install <u>VS Code</u>.

Step 2: Install AI Extensions

- GitHub Copilot: Install from VS Code Marketplace.

- Codeium: Install from VS Code Marketplace.

Step 3: Set Up API-based Tools (ChatGPT, Claude)

- Register for API keys from respective providers.

- Install API client plugins (like "ChatGPT: Genie AI" extension for VS Code).

Step 4: Test Your Integration

- Open VS Code. Type `function add(` and observe code suggestions.

- Ask your AI assistant via the integrated chat: *"Explain this code snippet."*

Integration Checklist:

- Installed VS Code

- Installed desired AI extensions

- Verified AI suggestions in the editor

- Set up API access for additional AI assistance

- Tested code generation and explanation features

Action Item:

- Integrate at least one AI tool into your VS Code today and test a simple JavaScript snippet.

Sample Exercises to Practice Integration:

Exercise 1: Quick Code Generation

Prompt your AI: "*Create a JavaScript function that checks if a number is prime.*"
Test and verify the AI-generated function in VS Code.

Exercise 2: Debugging Assistance

Paste faulty code into your AI:

```
let fruits = ["apple", "banana"];

console.log(fruit[2]);
```

Prompt: "*Fix and explain what's wrong.*"

Comprehensive Quiz: 25 Multiple Choice Questions

Question 1: Which AI tool is best for real-time code completion?
 A. ChatGPT
 B. GitHub Copilot ✓
 C. Claude
 D. Grammarly
Explanation: GitHub Copilot is designed specifically for real-time code suggestions.

Question 2: If you need detailed JavaScript explanations, you should use:
 A. GitHub Copilot
 B. ChatGPT or Claude ✓
 C. Codeium
 D. MS Word
Explanation: ChatGPT and Claude excel at detailed explanations and teaching.

Question 3: To integrate GitHub Copilot, you need:
 A. A printer
 B. VS Code editor and Copilot extension ✓
 C. Only Google Chrome
 D. Physical hardware
 Explanation: VS Code with the Copilot extension is necessary for integration.

Question 4: For writing repetitive JavaScript loops quickly, which AI tool is ideal?
 A. Claude
 B. ChatGPT
 C. GitHub Copilot ✓
 D. Grammarly
 Explanation: GitHub Copilot is designed for quickly handling repetitive coding tasks in real-time.

Question 5: Which task suits ChatGPT best?
 A. Real-time code completion
 B. Detailed code explanations ✓
 C. Hardware installations
 D. Cooking recipes
 Explanation: ChatGPT provides detailed, clear explanations of coding concepts.

Question 6: What's required for integrating AI tools into your editor?
 A. An API key (for some tools) ✓
 B. A physical AI device
 C. Special hardware
 D. A mobile phone
 Explanation: Many advanced AI tools require API keys for integration.

Question 7: Codeium excels at:
 A. Slow, detailed explanations
 B. Fast, real-time coding suggestions ✓
 C. Artistic creations
 D. Legal document generation
Explanation: Codeium provides fast, accurate coding suggestions during development.

Question 8: AI integration into VS Code typically involves:
 A. Installing VS Code extensions ✓
 B. Using physical hardware
 C. Learning a new spoken language
 D. Writing in a physical notebook
Explanation: VS Code extensions provide seamless integration with AI tools.

Question 9: Claude's strength primarily lies in:
 A. Detailed, accurate explanations and safe coding ✓
 B. Physical hardware troubleshooting
 C. Replacing all coding tasks
 D. Real-time code completion only
Explanation: Claude emphasizes high-quality, accurate explanations and safe, reliable code.

Question 10: Which tool would you use for rapid development sessions?
 A. Grammarly
 B. Codeium ✓
 C. MS Word
 D. Zoom
Explanation: Codeium is built specifically for high productivity during coding sessions.

Question 11: Effective use of AI tools requires:
 A. Physical presence of an AI robot
 B. Clear and structured prompts ✓
 C. Vague instructions
 D. Long essays
 Explanation: Clear and structured prompts enhance AI effectiveness significantly.

Question 12: Best AI tool for debugging code interactively:
 A. Grammarly
 B. ChatGPT or Claude ✓
 C. MS Excel
 D. Spotify
 Explanation: ChatGPT and Claude excel at debugging tasks interactively.

Question 13: Using GitHub Copilot primarily helps with:
 A. Writing creative literature
 B. Artistic drawing
 C. Real-time code snippet completion ✓
 D. Hardware repairs
 Explanation: GitHub Copilot provides automatic code completions directly in your code editor.

Question 14: A beginner-friendly AI tool offering detailed JavaScript teaching:
 A. Grammarly
 B. ChatGPT ✓
 C. MS Paint
 D. Photoshop
 Explanation: ChatGPT offers beginner-friendly explanations and examples for coding concepts.

Question 15: API keys are typically required for tools like:
A. GitHub Copilot
B. ChatGPT and Claude ✓
C. Microsoft Word
D. Spotify
Explanation: ChatGPT and Claude typically require API keys for integration.

Question 16: Integrating AI into existing workflows primarily benefits you by:
A. Eliminating the need for coding entirely
B. Saving time on repetitive tasks ✓
C. Automatically becoming an expert programmer
D. Never needing testing again
Explanation: AI integration helps primarily by handling repetitive coding tasks efficiently.

Question 17: Codeium integrates best with which tool?
A. Microsoft Word
B. VS Code ✓
C. Google Docs
D. Photoshop
Explanation: Codeium integrates smoothly and effectively into VS Code.

Question 18: Which AI tool would you choose for a quick JavaScript code generation directly in your editor?
A. ChatGPT
B. Claude
C. GitHub Copilot or Codeium ✓
D. Grammarly
Explanation: GitHub Copilot or Codeium provide direct, real-time code suggestions in editors.

Question 19: Claude is particularly good for:
 A. Real-time coding only
 B. Fast completion without explanations
 C. Detailed explanations and safe coding practices ✓
 D. Generating cooking recipes
Explanation: Claude specializes in detailed, reliable code and clear explanations.

Question 20: Best practice for using AI tools involves:
 A. Immediately using generated code without testing
 B. Thorough testing and verification ✓
 C. Avoiding AI completely
 D. Ignoring all human intervention
Explanation: Always thoroughly test and verify AI-generated code before use.

Question 21: Which AI tool helps most clearly explain JavaScript arrays to beginners?
 A. GitHub Copilot
 B. ChatGPT or Claude ✓
 C. Grammarly
 D. MS Excel
Explanation: ChatGPT and Claude offer clear, beginner-friendly explanations.

Question 22: What's essential for successful AI integration?
 A. Ignoring AI entirely
 B. Using vague instructions
 C. Precise prompts and thorough review ✓
 D. Avoiding AI outputs
Explanation: Precise prompts and careful review ensure successful AI integration.

Question 23: Which AI tool is least suited for real-time coding completions?
A. GitHub Copilot
B. Codeium
C. ChatGPT ✓
D. Grammarly
Explanation: ChatGPT is conversational and explanation-oriented, less ideal for real-time completions in the editor.

Question 24: Integrating AI coding tools into your environment mainly requires:
A. Installing specific editor plugins or extensions ✓
B. Buying expensive hardware
C. Completely stopping manual coding
D. Physical workspace adjustments
Explanation: AI coding tools are usually integrated via editor extensions or plugins.

Question 25: The primary goal of using AI in your JavaScript workflow is:
A. Completely replacing human coding
B. Avoiding learning JavaScript
C. Enhancing productivity and understanding ✓
D. Eliminating all testing
Explanation: The goal is enhancing productivity and helping you better understand JavaScript coding concepts.

Additional Action Items:

- Explore at least two more AI tools from the list above.

- Practice writing detailed prompts and compare AI outputs.

- Integrate one more AI tool into your workflow.

Chapter Conclusion:

Congratulations! You've now learned how to set up your AI coding toolkit, select the appropriate tool for various JavaScript tasks, and integrate these powerful assistants into your daily workflow. You're ready to enhance your coding productivity significantly, leveraging AI tools effectively.

Chapter 3: Prompting Like a Pro

As you start working more with AI to write JavaScript, your ability to provide clear, precise instructions—known as *prompting*—becomes incredibly important. This chapter will teach you how to craft effective prompts to get the most accurate, detailed, and useful results from your AI assistant.

Learning Objectives

By the end of this chapter, you will be able to:

- Clearly write precise developer prompts for AI tools.

- Build systematic prompts step-by-step, enhancing accuracy.

- Improve AI-generated outputs by asking for explanations, tests, and alternative solutions.

- Confidently practice and apply these prompting techniques to practical JavaScript tasks.

How to Write Clear and Precise Developer Prompts

Good prompting is essential. Think of your AI assistant as a new teammate who needs clear instructions to perform tasks effectively. Vague prompts produce vague results. Precise prompts produce precise, usable code.

Keys to Effective Prompts:

- **Be Specific:** Clearly state exactly what you want.

- **Include Examples:** Provide example inputs and expected outputs.

- **Clarify Context:** Give background or scenario details.

- **Define Constraints:** Specify requirements, limits, or special instructions clearly.

Example:

- **Vague Prompt:**
  "Write JavaScript code to do math."

- **Clear Prompt:**
  "Write a JavaScript function that takes two numbers and returns their sum, difference, product, and quotient as an object."

AI-generated Code from Clear Prompt:

```
function mathOperations(num1, num2) {

  return {

    sum: num1 + num2,

    difference: num1 - num2,

    product: num1 * num2,

    quotient: num2 !== 0 ? num1 / num2 :
"Cannot divide by zero"

  };

}
```

Exercise 1:

Rewrite this prompt clearly: *"Make a thing that finds if text is long."*
 (Example solution: *"Create a JavaScript function that checks if a given text string has more than 10 characters and returns true or false."*)

Systematic Prompting: Building Instructions Layer by Layer

Writing complex prompts can feel challenging. The solution is **systematic prompting**, breaking down requests into smaller, clear layers:

Steps for Systematic Prompting:

1. **Start Simple:** First, ask for basic functionality.

2. **Add Specifics:** Introduce constraints or details incrementally.

3. **Ask for Examples:** Request examples to verify correctness.

4. **Request Alternatives:** Ask AI to suggest alternate solutions or improvements.

Real-World Example:

1. **Initial Prompt:**
    "Write a JavaScript function that checks if a number is even."

2. **Layered Detail (Constraint):**
   "Now update the function to return a clear message like 'The number 4 is even'."

3. **Verification (Example):**
   "Provide two usage examples."

4. **Alternative Request:**
   "Suggest another way to write this function."

Exercise 2:

Use systematic prompting to create a JavaScript function that calculates the square root of a number and clearly handles negative inputs.

Getting Better Output: Asking for Explanations, Tests, and Alternatives

You can greatly improve your AI-generated JavaScript by explicitly requesting explanations, tests, and alternative approaches in your prompts.

Techniques for Enhanced Output:

- **Request Explanations:** Clarify logic and understanding.

- **Request Tests:** Ask for example test cases or verification code.

- **Request Alternatives:** Explore different ways to solve a problem.

Example Enhanced Prompt: *"Write a JavaScript function to reverse a string. Explain how it works, include two tests, and suggest an alternative approach."*

Sample AI-generated Response:

```
// Function using built-in methods

function reverseString(str) {

    return str.split('').reverse().join('');

}

// Explanation:

// split('') separates the string into an
array of characters.

// reverse() reverses the array order.

// join('') combines the reversed array back
into a single string.

// Tests:

console.log(reverseString("hello")); //
"olleh"

console.log(reverseString("world")); //
"dlrow"

// Alternative:

// Using a loop:

function reverseStringLoop(str) {

    let reversed = '';
```

```
  for(let i = str.length - 1; i >= 0; i--) {

    reversed += str[i];

  }

  return reversed;

}
```

Exercise 3:

Prompt your AI tool:
"Create a JavaScript function that checks if a year is a leap year. Include an explanation, two tests, and provide an alternative solution."

Checklist for Writing Effective Prompts:

- Clearly specify your goal.

- Include necessary details and constraints.

- Request an explanation to deepen understanding.

- Ask for example tests to verify correctness.

- Explore alternative solutions for flexibility.

Action Items for Practical Mastery:

- Practice rewriting vague prompts into precise, layered instructions.

- Regularly request explanations, tests, and alternatives from your AI tool.

- Create a library of proven effective prompts for future reference.

Comprehensive Quiz: 25 Multiple Choice Questions

Question 1: What's essential for effective AI prompting?
A. Using vague descriptions
B. Providing specific instructions ✓
C. Long, confusing sentences
D. Physical writing

Explanation: Specific instructions ensure clear, usable AI responses.

Question 2: Which step is key in systematic prompting?
A. Avoiding examples
B. Adding detail incrementally ✓
C. Skipping testing
D. Using random questions

Explanation: Incremental detail clarifies tasks, improving accuracy.

Question 3: Including examples in prompts helps AI by:
A. Making prompts confusing
B. Clearly showing expectations ✓
C. Eliminating AI use
D. Replacing human judgment

Explanation: Examples clarify what the AI should deliver.

Question 4:

Which prompt will produce better AI-generated code?
A. "Write some JavaScript."
B. "Write code."
C. "Make something happen."
D. "Create a JavaScript function to add two numbers and return the sum." ✓

Explanation: Option D clearly defines the desired outcome, enabling accurate AI responses.

Question 5:

What does systematic prompting involve?
A. One vague request
B. Multiple unrelated requests
C. Building instructions layer by layer ✓
D. Ignoring AI output

Explanation: Systematic prompting adds clarity by incrementally providing detailed instructions.

Question 6:

Why ask AI to include explanations with code?
A. To confuse the AI
B. To improve your understanding ✓
C. To slow down coding
D. To eliminate the need for testing

Explanation: Explanations deepen understanding of generated code.

Question 7:

When prompting AI, providing constraints helps by:
A. Making tasks unclear
B. Narrowing down solutions clearly ✓
C. Increasing ambiguity
D. Ignoring requirements

Explanation: Constraints clarify the exact parameters needed.

Question 8:

Which of the following improves AI output quality?
A. Providing examples and tests ✅
B. Being intentionally vague
C. Avoiding details
D. Keeping requests extremely broad

Explanation: Examples and tests help AI understand precisely what's needed.

Question 9:

The best way to request alternatives from AI is to:
A. Ask for exactly the same result repeatedly
B. Clearly request alternative solutions ✅
C. Make prompts shorter
D. Avoid prompting

Explanation: Explicitly asking for alternatives ensures varied and innovative solutions.

Question 10:

What's an effective prompt for debugging code?
A. "Something is wrong."
B. "Fix it."
C. "My code doesn't work, here's the exact error message..." ✅
D. "Code now!"

Explanation: Providing exact errors gives AI clear context for debugging.

Question 11:

Effective prompts for code generation should be:
 A. Broad and unspecific
 B. Clearly detailed and precise ✓
 C. Extremely long essays
 D. Random sentences

Explanation: Clear, detailed prompts yield precise AI outputs.

Question 12:

Systematic prompting helps AI primarily by:
 A. Making tasks harder
 B. Reducing confusion through clarity ✓
 C. Ignoring details
 D. Skipping testing

Explanation: Clarity from systematic prompting reduces AI confusion.

Question 13:

Prompting AI to generate test cases:
 A. Wastes time
 B. Ensures correctness and validation ✓
 C. Confuses the AI
 D. Eliminates AI output

Explanation: Test cases validate and ensure correct AI-generated code.

Question 14:

Asking AI for multiple code solutions helps by:
 A. Making tasks confusing
 B. Providing alternative approaches ✓
 C. Eliminating coding practice
 D. Reducing your choices

Explanation: Alternative solutions help find the best approach.

Question 15:

A systematic prompt starts by:
 A. Asking for everything at once
 B. Clearly stating a basic goal ✓
 C. Being intentionally vague
 D. Not stating anything clearly

Explanation: Starting with a clear, basic goal establishes a solid foundation.

Question 16:

Clear prompts significantly improve:
 A. Code efficiency and accuracy ✓
 B. AI confusion
 C. Ambiguity
 D. Difficulty

Explanation: Clarity greatly enhances AI-generated code quality.

Question 17:

Effective prompts typically include:
 A. Irrelevant details
 B. Clear instructions and constraints ✓
 C. Ambiguous language
 D. Random tasks

Explanation: Clear instructions and constraints guide AI effectively.

Question 18:

Good prompting technique involves:
 A. Always starting vague
 B. Incrementally adding details ✓
 C. Using one-word prompts
 D. Avoiding details entirely

Explanation: Incremental detailing enhances prompt effectiveness.

Question 19:

Asking AI for explanations is beneficial because it:
 A. Creates confusion
 B. Clarifies how code works ✓
 C. Prevents testing
 D. Speeds up hardware

Explanation: Explanations clarify AI-generated logic and improve understanding.

Question 20:

Requesting alternative methods in prompts helps you to:
 A. Have fewer options
 B. Explore different coding solutions ✓
 C. Ignore solutions
 D. Reduce clarity

Explanation: Alternatives let you discover potentially better coding solutions.

Question 21:

Systematic prompting encourages:
 A. Random requests
 B. Clarity and structured responses ✓
 C. Immediate confusion
 D. Fewer explanations

Explanation: Structured, clear prompts yield structured and accurate outputs.

Question 22:

AI-generated tests are important because they:
 A. Slow down coding
 B. Validate code correctness ✓
 C. Confuse beginners
 D. Eliminate coding

Explanation: Tests help ensure AI-generated code functions correctly.

Question 23:

What's the benefit of clearly stating constraints in prompts?
 A. Reduces accuracy
 B. Narrows AI's focus to correct solutions ✓
 C. Makes code worse
 D. Increases confusion

Explanation: Constraints guide AI precisely toward correct solutions.

Question 24:

Providing clear examples in prompts helps AI:
 A. Ignore instructions
 B. Understand exactly what's expected ✓
 C. Slow down processes
 D. Skip tests

Explanation: Examples illustrate clearly the expected outcomes.

Question 25:

Prompting for detailed explanations from AI is helpful for:
 A. Making tasks unclear
 B. Deepening your coding knowledge ✓
 C. Skipping testing entirely
 D. Avoiding AI altogether

Explanation: Detailed explanations enhance understanding and learning.

Sample Exercises Recap (Practice These):

- **Exercise 1 (Prompt Clarification):** Rewrite vague instructions clearly.

- **Exercise 2 (Systematic Prompting):** Layer prompts to build complex functions.

- **Exercise 3 (Enhanced Output):** Request explanations, tests, and alternatives.

Chapter Conclusion:

You've learned how to communicate clearly and effectively with AI coding tools. By systematically layering prompts, asking for clarifications, tests, and alternatives, you'll consistently receive high-quality JavaScript code. Practice these techniques regularly, and you'll master AI-assisted JavaScript development in no time.

Chapter 4: Writing Code with AI Assistance

In this chapter, you'll learn how to harness AI as your coding partner to create, improve, and build JavaScript projects. Even if you've never written code before, you'll find AI an incredibly helpful collaborator.

Learning Objectives

By the end of this chapter, you will:

- Understand how to co-write JavaScript components and functions using AI.

- Use AI to refactor and improve existing JavaScript codebases.

- Effectively describe coding requirements to AI for accurate results.

- Apply practical AI-assisted techniques to write cleaner, more efficient JavaScript code.

How to Co-Write Components and Functions

Coding doesn't have to be intimidating—especially when you're co-writing JavaScript functions with AI. Think of AI as your teammate who translates your ideas into code instantly.

Step-by-Step Approach to Co-Writing:

1. **Describe your goal clearly:** Explain what the code should achieve.

2. **Request specific JavaScript code:** Clearly ask for functions or components.

3. **Review and test generated code:** Always check that the output meets your expectations.

Example: Creating a Simple Greeting Component

Clear Prompt:

"Create a JavaScript function named `greetUser` that takes a user's name and returns 'Hello, [name]!' as a greeting."

AI-generated code:

```
function greetUser(name) {
   return `Hello, ${name}!`;
}
```

Testing the function:

```
console.log(greetUser("Alex"));  // Output:
Hello, Alex!
```

Exercise 1:

Use AI to co-write a JavaScript function called `multiplyNumbers` that takes two numbers and returns their product.
Prompt Example: "Write a JavaScript function called `multiplyNumbers` that multiplies two numbers."

Using AI to Refactor Old Codebases

Refactoring means improving existing code without changing its functionality. AI makes this process easy, even if you're new to coding.

When Should You Refactor?

- When code feels repetitive or unclear.

- When code needs optimization for better performance.

- When improving readability for easier maintenance.

Real-World Example: Refactoring for Readability

Old code:

```
function calculateArea(w,h){
return w*h
}
```

Prompt to AI:

> "Refactor this JavaScript function to improve readability and add clear comments."

AI Refactored Code:

```
// Calculate the area of a rectangle given width and height
function calculateArea(width, height) {
  return width * height; // Returns the area
}
```

Refactoring Checklist:

- Identify unclear or inefficient code.

- Prompt AI clearly to refactor for readability or performance.

- Review and test AI's improved code thoroughly.

Exercise 2:

Use AI to refactor this code snippet for clarity:

```
let s=0;for(let
i=1;i<=5;i++){s+=i;}console.log(s);
```

Building from Requirements: How to Describe What You Want

Clearly defining your requirements ensures the AI accurately transforms your idea into JavaScript code.

Guidelines for Effective Requirements:

- Clearly state the main goal or task.

- Describe expected inputs and outputs.

- Include examples of intended results.

Example: Creating a To-Do List Component

Prompt Example:

> "Create a JavaScript function called addTodoItem. It should take an array and a string as inputs, add the string to the array, and return the updated array. Provide an example usage."

AI-generated Response:

```javascript
// Adds a new to-do item to the existing
list
function addTodoItem(todoList, newItem) {
  todoList.push(newItem); // Adds the new
item to the array
  return todoList; // Returns the updated
list
}
// Example usage:
let myTodos = ["Learn JavaScript", "Practice
AI prompting"];
console.log(addTodoItem(myTodos, "Build a
website"));
// Output: ["Learn JavaScript", "Practice AI
prompting", "Build a website"]
```

Exercise 3:

Clearly describe to AI how to build a function named
checkEvenOrOdd that determines if a number is even or
odd, returning a clear message like "Number 4 is even."

Action Items for Practical Mastery:

- Practice daily AI-assisted co-writing of JavaScript
  functions.

- Regularly identify code snippets for refactoring with
  AI.

- Clearly define and communicate your coding
  requirements to AI.

Multiple Choice Quiz (10 Questions):

Question 1: What does "refactoring" mean in coding?

- A. Adding new features

- B. Deleting all existing code

- C. Improving existing code without changing functionality ✓

- D. Writing code from scratch
  Explanation: Refactoring involves enhancing existing code's structure and readability without altering its behavior.

Question 2: Effective AI co-writing involves:

- A. Providing vague ideas

- B. Clearly describing your coding goal ✓

- C. Ignoring AI output

- D. Never testing code
  Explanation: Clear descriptions ensure accurate AI-generated code.

Question 3: When describing requirements, it's best to:

- A. Avoid specifics

- B. Include examples of inputs and expected outputs ✓

- C. Give random instructions

- D. Use unclear language
  Explanation: Examples clarify exactly what you expect from AI-generated solutions.

Question 4: Why test AI-generated code?

- A. AI code never works initially

- B. Ensures the code meets your expectations ✅

- C. To confuse yourself

- D. Because AI can't write code
  Explanation: Testing confirms the AI-generated code matches your intent.

Question 5: Refactoring with AI helps you to:

- A. Slow down development

- B. Confuse your teammates

- C. Improve readability and efficiency ✅

- D. Avoid testing entirely
  Explanation: AI helps improve code quality quickly and efficiently.

Question 6: Which prompt is clear and effective?

- A. "Make a thing."

- B. "Write JavaScript."

- C. "Create a JavaScript function to reverse a string." ✓

- D. "Code now!"
  Explanation: Clear prompts like option C yield precise results.

Question 7: The main benefit of co-writing with AI is:

- A. No need to test code

- B. Increased productivity and learning ✓

- C. Completely eliminates coding

- D. More confusion
  Explanation: Co-writing improves productivity and supports learning by example.

Question 8: How do you verify refactored code is correct?

- A. Assume it's perfect

- B. Run tests and review carefully ✓

- C. Avoid using it

- D. Copy-paste without checks
  Explanation: Always verify code changes through tests and careful review.

Question 9: What's essential in your requirements description?

- A. Vague statements

- B. Random details

- C. Clear goals and examples ✓

- D. Very lengthy descriptions
  Explanation: Clear goals and specific examples enhance AI accuracy.

Question 10: The best way to learn from AI-generated code is to:

- A. Ignore it completely

- B. Always request explanations and tests ✓

- C. Never test the code

- D. Avoid reading it
  Explanation: Explanations and tests reinforce your understanding.

Chapter Conclusion:

You've learned how to effectively collaborate with AI to co-write JavaScript components, refactor existing code, and build clearly defined solutions from your requirements. With regular practice, you'll find yourself confidently creating and improving JavaScript projects, empowered by your AI assistant.

Chapter 5: Debugging and Troubleshooting with AI

Debugging can feel intimidating, especially if you're new to coding. Thankfully, AI makes it easier. In this chapter, you'll learn how to leverage AI to troubleshoot JavaScript errors effectively, identify the root causes of unexpected behavior, and build practical debugging playbooks.

Learning Objectives

By the end of this chapter, you will be able to:

- Clearly communicate JavaScript errors and unexpected behavior to AI.

- Use AI to interpret stack traces and error messages effectively.

- Collaborate with AI to systematically identify root causes of problems.

- Create structured debugging playbooks using AI to resolve issues efficiently.

Feeding AI Errors, Stack Traces, and Unexpected Behavior

When your JavaScript code doesn't work as expected, AI can quickly help diagnose what's going wrong. The key is clearly feeding AI the exact errors or unexpected behaviors.

How to Describe Errors to AI Effectively:

1. **Copy and Paste the Exact Error Message:**
   Always include exact wording of the error.

2. **Include Your Code Snippet:**
   Provide the code causing the error.

3. **Explain Expected vs. Actual Behavior:**
   Describe clearly what you expected the code to do and what it's doing instead.

Example: Diagnosing a Common Error

Suppose you have the following JavaScript code:

```
let numbers = [1, 2, 3];
console.log(numbers[3]);
```

This outputs:

```
undefined
```

Prompting AI:

> "Why am I getting `undefined` when I try to access `numbers[3]`?"

AI Response:

> "JavaScript arrays start at index 0, so `numbers[3]` refers to a fourth element that doesn't exist. Your array has indexes 0, 1, and 2. Thus, accessing index 3 returns `undefined`."

Exercise 1:

Run this code snippet and ask AI why you receive an error:

```
function greet(name) {
```

```
  console.log("Hello, " + name);
}
greet();
```

How to Collaborate with AI to Identify Root Causes

Collaborating with AI means engaging in a structured conversation to dig deeper into the issue.

Steps for AI Collaboration:

1. **Present the Initial Problem Clearly:**
    Clearly explain the initial symptoms or errors.

2. **Request a Detailed Explanation:**
    Ask AI why this error might be occurring.

3. **Iterate with Additional Details:**
    Provide further context if the initial response doesn't fully clarify.

Real-world Example:

Consider this problematic code snippet:

```
let total = 0;
for (let i = 1; i <= 5; i++) {
  total += i;
}
console.log(total);
console.log(i);
```

The second `console.log(i);` throws an error.

Prompting AI:

"Why does the second `console.log(i);` throw an error?"

AI Response:

"The variable `i` is defined with `let` inside the for-loop, which restricts its scope to the loop itself. Accessing it outside the loop causes a ReferenceError."

Exercise 2:

Use AI to determine the root cause of this unexpected result:

```
let result = "5" + 10;
console.log(result);
```

Building Debugging Playbooks

Debugging playbooks are step-by-step guides to solving common issues. With AI, you can quickly generate structured debugging playbooks.

Creating Your Debugging Playbook:

- **Identify Common Errors:** Note frequent issues.

- **Use AI to Explain Causes and Solutions:** Prompt AI for clear, structured explanations.

- **Document Steps Clearly:** Record AI's guidance step-by-step for future reference.

Example Playbook: Fixing "undefined" Errors in Arrays

Step 1: Verify array length vs. accessed index.
Step 2: Adjust indexing if exceeding length.
Step 3: Check if arrays are populated correctly.

AI-generated Detailed Playbook:

Prompt:

> "Create a detailed debugging playbook to fix JavaScript 'undefined' errors when accessing array elements."

AI Response:

1. **Check array indices:** JavaScript arrays start at 0, so ensure you're accessing within array length.

2. **Validate array population:** Ensure your array has elements before accessing them.

3. **Use conditional checks:** Implement `if` statements to avoid accessing non-existent elements.

Checklist for Effective Debugging:

- Clearly state the exact error or unexpected result.

- Include code causing the issue.

- Request detailed explanations from AI.

- Create structured steps for resolving similar future issues.

Action Items for Practical Mastery:

- Practice regularly feeding clear errors and stack traces into your AI assistant.

- Engage in iterative conversations with AI to explore root causes.

- Create personalized debugging playbooks for common issues.

Multiple Choice Quiz (10 Questions):

Question 1: Why should you copy exact errors into AI prompts?

- A. To confuse AI

- B. Ensures accurate diagnosis ✓

- C. Speeds up coding

- D. Avoids testing
  Explanation: Exact errors help AI precisely identify the issue.

Question 2: What's an effective debugging approach with AI?

- A. Provide vague descriptions

- B. Clearly state symptoms and code ✓

- C. Ignore AI suggestions

- D. Avoid details
  Explanation: Clearly stating the issue ensures accurate AI solutions.

Question 3: Why does `console.log(numbers[3])` return undefined for `[1,2,3]`?

- A. Array indexing starts at 1

- B. The array has only three elements indexed 0–2 ✅

- C. Arrays cannot store numbers

- D. JavaScript forbids accessing arrays
  Explanation: Arrays index from 0, so index 3 doesn't exist for this array.

Question 4: The key benefit of a debugging playbook is:

- A. Rewriting code entirely

- B. Structured, repeatable solutions ✅

- C. Ignoring issues

- D. Avoiding AI assistance
  Explanation: Playbooks provide structured solutions for repeated use.

Question 5: Effective AI collaboration involves:

- A. Immediate single-step answers only

- B. Iterative questioning for deeper insight ✅

- C. Vague questioning

- D. Avoiding details
  Explanation: Iterative questioning helps AI clarify and identify root causes.

Question 6: What causes the error when accessing a `let` variable outside its block?

- A. Variables don't exist in JavaScript

- B. `let` variables have limited scope ✓

- C. JavaScript forbids variables

- D. `let` is always global
  Explanation: Variables declared with `let` exist only within their defined block.

Question 7: What does the AI debugging checklist help you do?

- A. Write vague errors

- B. Skip testing

- C. Clearly structure your debugging process ✓

- D. Slow down work
  Explanation: A structured process ensures efficient debugging.

Question 8: What's essential when describing unexpected behaviors to AI?

- A. No context or details

- B. Precise expected vs actual behavior ✓

- C. Single-word prompts

- D. Long unrelated essays
  Explanation: Clearly stating expected vs actual helps AI diagnose accurately.

Question 9: When should you refactor code using AI?

- A. When code works perfectly

- B. When code is unclear or repetitive ✓

- C. To confuse your team

- D. Avoiding tests
  Explanation: Refactor unclear or repetitive code for readability and efficiency.

Question 10: A debugging playbook typically includes:

- A. Random unrelated solutions

- B. Structured troubleshooting steps ✓

- C. Vague descriptions

- D. No solutions
  Explanation: Structured steps clearly guide troubleshooting processes.

Chapter Conclusion:

You've learned essential debugging techniques using AI, from clearly describing problems to collaborating iteratively and building structured debugging playbooks. Continue practicing these strategies, and you'll confidently handle JavaScript errors and unexpected behaviors with ease and clarity.

Chapter 6: Generating and Improving Tests

Testing is a crucial part of creating reliable, error-free JavaScript code. Even if you're new to coding, you can easily leverage AI to generate high-quality tests that cover different scenarios, including those tricky edge cases. In this chapter, you'll learn how to use AI effectively to write various types of tests and generate mock data rapidly.

Learning Objectives

By the end of this chapter, you will be able to:

- Use AI to generate unit, integration, and end-to-end (E2E) tests for JavaScript.

- Prompt AI effectively to ensure your tests cover important edge cases.

- Quickly generate realistic mock data and test scenarios using AI.

- Apply practical AI-assisted testing strategies to enhance your code quality and reliability.

Using AI to Write Unit, Integration, and E2E Tests

Let's first understand the basics of these three important test types:

- **Unit tests:** Test individual components or functions to ensure they work correctly in isolation.

- **Integration tests:** Check if multiple parts of your application work together as expected.

- **End-to-End (E2E) tests:** Simulate real user interactions with your complete application, ensuring everything functions from start to finish.

Writing Clear Prompts for Tests

To get AI to write effective tests, provide clear instructions including:

- The specific component or function to test.

- Desired test scenarios.

- Examples of expected outcomes.

Example: Writing a Unit Test with AI

JavaScript function to test:

```
function add(a, b) {
  return a + b;
}
```

Prompt to AI:

> "Write unit tests in JavaScript using Jest for this add function. Include tests for regular and edge cases."

AI-generated Tests:

```
// Jest tests for add function
test('adds two positive numbers correctly',
() => {
```

```
  expect(add(2, 3)).toBe(5);
});
test('adds negative numbers correctly', ()
=> {
  expect(add(-2, -3)).toBe(-5);
});
test('handles zero correctly', () => {
  expect(add(0, 0)).toBe(0);
});
```

Exercise 1:

Use AI to generate unit tests for a function named multiply, which multiplies two numbers.

How to Ask AI to Cover Edge Cases You Might Miss

Edge cases are scenarios that occur under extreme or unexpected conditions. They are important to test because they often cause unexpected bugs.

Prompting AI for Edge Cases:

- Explicitly request edge cases and unusual scenarios.

- Ask AI to suggest edge cases you may not think of yourself.

Example: Identifying Edge Cases with AI

Prompt Example:

> "List possible edge cases for a JavaScript function that divides two numbers."

AI Response:

- Dividing by zero

- Dividing very large numbers

- Dividing negative numbers

- Dividing non-numeric inputs

Checklist for Covering Edge Cases:

- Clearly define your function.

- Ask AI explicitly for potential edge cases.

- Generate tests covering each edge case.

Exercise 2:

Prompt AI to provide edge cases and tests for a function named `isAdult(age)` that returns true if age is 18 or greater.

Generating Mock Data and Test Scenarios Fast

Realistic mock data helps you thoroughly test your application. AI can rapidly generate diverse and realistic data sets to test various scenarios.

How to Prompt AI for Mock Data:

- Clearly describe what kind of data you need (e.g., names, dates, numbers).

- Specify quantity and variations required.

Example: Generating Mock User Data

Prompt:

> "Generate mock user data including first name,
> last name, email, and age for three users."

AI-generated Data:

```
const users = [
  { firstName: "John", lastName: "Doe",
email: "john.doe@example.com", age: 28 },
  { firstName: "Jane", lastName: "Smith",
email: "jane.smith@example.com", age: 34 },
  { firstName: "Alice", lastName: "Johnson",
email: "alice.johnson@example.com", age: 45
}
];
```

Exercise 3:

Prompt AI to generate mock data for five product items,
each having a name, price, and quantity.

Action Items for Practical Mastery:

- Regularly use AI to generate tests for every new
  JavaScript function you create.

- Request edge cases explicitly from AI for thorough
  test coverage.

- Frequently use AI-generated mock data to test
  realistic scenarios.

Multiple Choice Quiz (10 Questions):

Question 1: What is a unit test?

- A. Tests multiple functions together

- B. Tests a whole application

- C. Tests an individual function or component ✓

- D. Tests the user interface only
  Explanation: Unit tests verify the correctness of individual units or functions in isolation.

Question 2: Integration tests are designed to:

- A. Verify individual functions separately

- B. Check interactions between different parts of an application ✓

- C. Test only visual components

- D. Replace user testing completely
  Explanation: Integration tests ensure different parts work together correctly.

Question 3: End-to-end (E2E) tests are used for:

- A. Testing single functions

- B. Testing user flows from start to finish ✓

- C. Checking code syntax

- D. Avoiding unit testing
  Explanation: E2E tests simulate full user experiences through the entire application.

Question 4: Edge cases are:

- A. Always common scenarios

- B. Typical cases that always occur

- C. Unusual or extreme conditions not regularly considered ✓

- D. Tests that avoid real scenarios
  Explanation: Edge cases test unexpected or extreme conditions that could cause bugs.

Question 5: The best way to identify edge cases with AI is to:

- A. Avoid prompting specifically

- B. Clearly ask AI to list potential edge cases ✓

- C. Never test them

- D. Test common cases only
  Explanation: Explicitly asking AI ensures thorough consideration of possible edge cases.

Question 6: Mock data helps by:

- A. Slowing down tests

- B. Providing unrealistic examples

- C. Testing real-life scenarios realistically ✓

- D. Ignoring important tests
  Explanation: Mock data allows realistic scenario testing without using real user data.

Question 7: AI-generated tests are beneficial because they:

- A. Increase manual work

- B. Quickly provide diverse test scenarios ✓

- C. Replace human judgment entirely

- D. Avoid finding errors
  Explanation: AI rapidly provides diverse scenarios and detailed tests.

Question 8: Why include clear examples in test prompts?

- A. To confuse AI

- B. Ensure AI precisely understands testing needs ✓

- C. Reduce accuracy

- D. Speed up testing by skipping examples
  Explanation: Clear examples guide AI in generating accurate tests.

Question 9: What does a good AI-generated testing prompt include?

- A. Vague instructions

- B. Clear function details and testing scenarios ✓

- C. Random ideas

- D. Ambiguous statements
  Explanation: Clear prompts generate precise and effective tests.

Question 10: Using AI for testing primarily helps you to:

- A. Avoid testing entirely

- B. Quickly generate high-quality tests ✓

- C. Slow down development

- D. Write longer code
  Explanation: AI accelerates generating comprehensive, reliable tests.

Chapter Conclusion:

You've now mastered how to effectively use AI to generate robust tests, cover important edge cases, and create realistic mock data quickly. Keep practicing these skills, and you'll consistently deliver high-quality JavaScript applications confidently and efficiently.

Chapter 7: Rapid Prototyping with AI

Creating prototypes quickly can dramatically accelerate your ability to turn ideas into reality. In this chapter, you'll learn how to leverage AI to rapidly build Minimum Viable Products (MVPs), demos, and Proofs of Concept (PoCs). You'll also discover how to explore different architectural approaches effectively using AI, and how to turn a simple idea into a working frontend in just one day.

Learning Objectives

By the end of this chapter, you will be able to:

- Understand how to rapidly prototype MVPs, demos, and PoCs using AI.

- Leverage AI to explore various architectural options for your JavaScript projects.

- Turn your project ideas into functional frontend applications quickly and efficiently.

- Confidently practice rapid prototyping techniques and apply them practically.

Building MVPs, Demos, and PoCs in Hours, Not Weeks

What is rapid prototyping?

Rapid prototyping involves quickly building a simplified version of your product or feature. It helps you:

- Test ideas fast.

- Gather early user feedback.

- Reduce overall development time and cost.

AI greatly enhances your ability to prototype rapidly, especially when coding with JavaScript.

How to Use AI for Rapid Prototyping:

Step-by-Step Process:

1. **Clearly Describe Your Idea:**
   Outline the core features or functions you want.

2. **Request AI to Generate an Initial Prototype:**
   Prompt AI clearly to produce basic code or components.

3. **Iterate Quickly:**
   Improve upon the AI-generated prototype based on feedback or further prompts.

Real-World Example:

Idea: A simple weather application that shows current temperature based on city input.

Prompt to AI:

"Create JavaScript code using Fetch API to get weather data from OpenWeatherMap API for a given city."

AI-generated prototype code:

```
async function getWeather(city) {
  const apiKey = 'your-api-key';
  const response = await
fetch(`https://api.openweathermap.org/data/2
.5/weather?q=${city}&appid=${apiKey}&units=m
etric`);
  const data = await response.json();
  console.log(`Temperature in ${city}:
${data.main.temp}°C`);
}
// Usage example
getWeather('London');
```

Exercise 1:

Use AI to create a simple JavaScript prototype that displays random motivational quotes from an array.

Leveraging AI to Explore Different Architectural Approaches

AI helps you explore and compare different ways to structure your JavaScript application architecture rapidly, even as a beginner.

How to Prompt AI for Architectural Suggestions:

- Clearly explain your project goal.

- Ask AI explicitly for architectural recommendations.

- Request pros and cons of different approaches.

Example: Architectural Recommendations

Prompt Example:

"Suggest two architectural approaches for building a simple JavaScript to-do list app and explain their pros and cons."

AI Response:

Approach 1: Vanilla JavaScript

- **Pros:** Simple, lightweight, easy to start quickly.

- **Cons:** Less scalable, harder to maintain for larger apps.

Approach 2: React Framework

- **Pros:** Scalable, easy component management, large community support.

- **Cons:** Slightly higher initial complexity for complete beginners.

Checklist for Evaluating AI-generated Architectures:

- Clearly define project requirements.

- Request multiple architectural approaches from AI.

- Review pros and cons.

- Select the best-fit architecture based on your goals.

Exercise 2:

Ask AI to provide two architectural options for a simple note-taking application and choose the best option based on its advice.

Example: From Idea to Working Frontend in a Day

Let's walk through a real-world scenario to demonstrate rapid prototyping from scratch to working frontend using AI within one day.

Scenario: Building a Simple Portfolio Webpage

Step 1: Define your goal clearly.
 Create a simple portfolio webpage with sections: "About Me," "Projects," and "Contact."

Step 2: Prompt AI for HTML structure.
 Request basic HTML code for your layout.

Prompt:

> "Generate basic HTML structure for a simple portfolio page with About Me, Projects, and Contact sections."

Step 3: Add styling quickly using AI.
 Ask AI for basic CSS to enhance appearance.

Prompt:

> "Provide simple CSS styles for this portfolio layout."

Step 4: Include JavaScript functionality using AI.
 Add interactivity, such as toggling visibility of sections.

Prompt:

> "Create simple JavaScript to toggle visibility of the Projects section when a button is clicked."

Exercise 3:

Follow the steps above to create your own simple interactive webpage for showcasing your favorite hobbies.

Action Items for Practical Mastery:

- Regularly practice building small, functional prototypes using AI.

- Frequently request and compare multiple architectural suggestions from AI.

- Complete mini-projects using the rapid prototyping workflow.

Multiple Choice Quiz (10 Questions):

Question 1: What is the primary goal of rapid prototyping?

- A. To build complete final products immediately

- B. Quickly testing and validating ideas ✓

- C. Avoiding user feedback

- D. Skipping coding entirely
  Explanation: Rapid prototyping allows quick idea validation and early feedback gathering.

Question 2: MVP stands for:

- A. Maximum Valuable Product

- B. Minimum Viable Product ✓

- C. Most Viewed Product

- D. Multiple Version Product
  Explanation: MVP is the smallest functional version of a product built quickly for testing.

Question 3: A Proof of Concept (PoC) is designed to:

- A. Prove an idea's feasibility ✓

- B. Replace detailed user testing

- C. Complete final application

- D. Ignore market validation
  Explanation: A PoC demonstrates that a certain idea or method works effectively.

Question 4: The advantage of using AI for prototyping is:

- A. Longer development time

- B. Rapid generation of basic working models ✓

- C. Eliminating all coding

- D. Avoiding feedback entirely
  Explanation: AI helps quickly produce workable code for rapid iteration and validation.

Question 5: When exploring architectures, you should:

- A. Avoid reviewing options

- B. Prompt AI clearly for multiple suggestions ✓

- C. Ignore scalability

- D. Skip evaluation entirely
  Explanation: AI helps compare multiple approaches to select the best fit for your project.

Question 6: Which scenario benefits most from rapid prototyping?

- A. Large-scale, detailed final products

- B. Quickly validating and iterating ideas ✓

- C. Avoiding user interaction

- D. Skipping code testing
  Explanation: Rapid prototyping is ideal for quick validation and iteration of ideas.

Question 7: Effective AI prompts for prototypes clearly state:

- A. Random ideas

- B. Vague descriptions

- C. Specific functionality and structure desired ✓

- D. Lengthy unrelated details
  Explanation: Clearly defined prompts yield accurate, functional prototypes quickly.

Question 8: A demo primarily serves to:

- A. Replace final products

- B. Demonstrate basic functionality quickly ✅

- C. Eliminate user testing

- D. Ignore feedback
  Explanation: Demos quickly showcase basic functionality for immediate feedback.

Question 9: What is essential when selecting an architecture suggested by AI?

- A. Ignoring AI recommendations

- B. Reviewing provided pros and cons carefully ✅

- C. Avoiding detailed review

- D. Random selection
  Explanation: Carefully reviewing pros and cons helps make an informed decision.

Question 10: From idea to working frontend quickly involves:

- A. Detailed planning and no coding

- B. Clear prompts and iterative AI usage ✅

- C. Avoiding all user feedback

- D. Writing extensive initial documentation
  Explanation: Rapid iteration with clear prompts ensures quick frontend development.

Chapter Conclusion:

You've mastered rapid prototyping techniques with AI, learning how to quickly build MVPs, demos, and PoCs, explore architectural options efficiently, and transform simple ideas into functional frontends in no time. Continue practicing these techniques, and you'll find yourself confidently bringing your JavaScript project ideas to life swiftly and effectively.

Chapter 8: Documentation and Code Comments

Clear documentation and informative code comments are crucial to maintaining readable, understandable, and manageable JavaScript code. Thankfully, AI makes documentation effortless — even for beginners. This chapter will teach you how to leverage AI to create helpful documentation and insightful comments automatically, helping you keep your projects clear and accessible.

Learning Objectives

By the end of this chapter, you will be able to:

- Use AI effectively to document your JavaScript code as you write.

- Generate comprehensive API documentation, clear code summaries, and helpful diagrams using AI.

- Keep your documentation accurately aligned with your codebase using AI assistance.

- Practically apply AI techniques to ensure your JavaScript code is always well-documented and understandable.

Getting AI to Document As You Code

Writing documentation as you code often seems tedious, but AI can simplify this process dramatically. AI-generated comments provide clarity and context, ensuring your code remains understandable for you and others.

How to Prompt AI for Effective Comments and Documentation:

- Clearly paste your JavaScript code snippet.

- Ask AI explicitly to generate descriptive comments or explanations.

Real-World Example: AI-Generated Comments

Original JavaScript Code:

```
function calculateDiscount(price,
discountPercent) {
  return price - (price * discountPercent /
100);
}
```

Prompt to AI:

> "Add clear, detailed comments explaining exactly what this JavaScript function does."

AI-generated Comments:

```
// This function calculates the discounted
price.
// Parameters:
// - price: original price before discount
// - discountPercent: discount percentage to
apply
function calculateDiscount(price,
discountPercent) {
  // Calculate discounted amount by
subtracting the percentage discount from the
original price
```

```
    return price - (price * discountPercent /
100);
}
```

Exercise 1:

Use AI to add detailed comments explaining the following code snippet:

```
function reverseString(str) {
    return str.split('').reverse().join('');
}
```

Using AI to Create API Documentation, Code Summaries, and Diagrams

Beyond comments, AI excels at generating comprehensive API documentation, concise code summaries, and clear visual diagrams. This helps anyone quickly understand how your JavaScript code works.

How to Prompt AI for Documentation and Diagrams:

- Clearly provide your code or describe your API functions.

- Request specific documentation formats (API docs, summaries, diagrams).

Example: AI-generated API Documentation

JavaScript API Function:

```
// Adds two numbers together
function add(a, b) {
    return a + b;
}
```

Prompt to AI:

> "Create simple API documentation for the add function."

AI-generated API Docs:

```
Function: add(a, b)
Description:
Returns the sum of two numbers provided as
arguments.
Parameters:
- a (Number): The first number.
- b (Number): The second number.
Returns:
- Number: The sum of a and b.
Example:
add(2, 3); // returns 5
```

Checklist for Effective AI Documentation:

- Clearly provide your JavaScript function or code snippet.

- Request specific documentation formats.

- Verify generated documentation for accuracy.

Exercise 2:

Prompt AI to create clear API documentation for a function named isPrime that checks if a number is prime.

Keeping Docs and Code Aligned with AI Help

Documentation quickly becomes outdated if not regularly maintained. AI helps keep documentation accurate and aligned with the latest version of your code.

How to Maintain Documentation with AI:

- Regularly request AI to review existing documentation and identify mismatches.

- Prompt AI to update documentation based on recent code changes.

Example: Updating Documentation with AI

Old Documentation:

```
Function: multiply(a, b)
Returns the product of two numbers.
```

Updated Code:

```
function multiply(a, b, c = 1) {
   return a * b * c;
}
```

Prompt to AI:

"Update documentation for this function based on recent changes."

Updated AI-generated Documentation:

```
Function: multiply(a, b, c = 1)
Description:
Returns the product of two or three numbers
provided as arguments. If the third argument
isn't provided, it defaults to 1.
Parameters:
```

```
- a (Number): The first number.
- b (Number): The second number.
- c (Number, optional): The third number,
default is 1.
Returns:
- Number: The product of a, b, and c.
Example:
multiply(2, 3); // returns 6
multiply(2, 3, 4); // returns 24
```

Exercise 3:

Use AI to update documentation based on this updated
JavaScript function:

Original Documentation:

```
Function: greetUser(name)
Returns a simple greeting message.
```

Updated Code:

```javascript
function greetUser(name, greeting = "Hello")
{
    return `${greeting}, ${name}!`;
}
```

Action Items for Practical Mastery:

- Regularly use AI to automatically generate comments
  and API documentation as you code.

- Consistently update your documentation to reflect
  code changes using AI.

- Build the habit of verifying AI-generated
  documentation accuracy and clarity.

Multiple Choice Quiz (10 Questions):

Question 1: Why use AI to document your code?

- A. To complicate your project

- B. To keep your code clear and understandable ✓

- C. To skip testing entirely

- D. To slow down development
  Explanation: AI simplifies documentation, ensuring clarity and maintainability.

Question 2: API documentation is useful primarily because it:

- A. Avoids describing your functions

- B. Clearly explains how to use your functions ✓

- C. Slows development

- D. Confuses users
  Explanation: API documentation clearly instructs users how to interact with your functions.

Question 3: Clear code comments help to:

- A. Confuse readers

- B. Clarify functionality quickly ✓

- C. Avoid testing

- D. Slow down the application
  Explanation: Comments provide quick context and clarity about your code's purpose.

Question 4: Effective AI documentation prompts clearly include:

- A. Random instructions

- B. Specific code and desired documentation formats ✓

- C. No examples

- D. Lengthy unrelated details
  Explanation: Specific prompts yield precise, accurate documentation.

Question 5: Diagrams generated by AI primarily:

- A. Complicate understanding

- B. Visually clarify complex logic ✓

- C. Replace all code

- D. Slow down reading
  Explanation: Diagrams simplify understanding of complex structures and interactions.

Question 6: Maintaining documentation with AI ensures:

- A. Outdated documentation

- B. Documentation stays accurate and aligned ✓

- C. Confusing information

- D. Avoiding updates entirely
  Explanation: Regular AI-assisted updates keep documentation accurate and relevant.

Question 7: Which documentation clearly states inputs and outputs?

- A. Ambiguous documentation

- B. API documentation ✓

- C. Irrelevant documentation

- D. Random notes
  Explanation: API documentation explicitly details function inputs and outputs.

Question 8: AI-generated summaries help by:

- A. Ignoring critical details

- B. Concisely explaining code purpose ✓

- C. Avoiding descriptions

- D. Slowing project understanding
  Explanation: Summaries offer quick, clear insights into code functionality.

Question 9: How often should you update documentation?

- A. Only at project start

- B. Regularly with code changes ✓

- C. Once yearly

- D. Never
  Explanation: Frequent updates keep documentation accurate and relevant.

Question 10: Good documentation primarily helps:

- A. Slow down team productivity

- B. Improve project maintainability and clarity ✓

- C. Avoid testing entirely

- D. Complicate user experience
  Explanation: Documentation greatly improves clarity, ease of maintenance, and teamwork efficiency.

Chapter Conclusion:

Fantastic work! You've learned how AI simplifies the process of documenting your JavaScript code effectively, maintaining clear, accurate documentation, and ensuring your code is understandable and maintainable. Continue leveraging these skills, and you'll find managing and explaining your projects a breeze.

Chapter 9: AI-Assisted Research and Learning

Learning JavaScript (and all that comes with it) can feel overwhelming. There are always new frameworks, tools, libraries, and best practices to stay on top of. The good news? AI is your secret weapon—not just for writing code, but also for learning more efficiently and staying informed without burnout. In this chapter, you'll discover how to use AI to accelerate your learning, explore new technologies, and stay current in the JavaScript world—without drowning in information.

Learning Objectives

By the end of this chapter, you will be able to:

- Use AI to speed up research on JavaScript frameworks, APIs, and best practices.

- Learn new technologies by prompting AI to act as your personal guide.

- Stay up-to-date with the ever-changing JavaScript landscape without becoming overwhelmed.

- Apply AI-assisted techniques to support continuous, targeted learning.

Speeding Up Research (Frameworks, APIs, Best Practices)

JavaScript is a fast-evolving language with hundreds of libraries and tools. When you're trying to figure out which framework to use or how to approach a problem, AI can help you filter the noise and get straight to what matters.

How AI Accelerates Research:

- **Summarizing documentation**: AI can quickly break down long docs into understandable summaries.

- **Comparing frameworks or libraries**: You can ask AI to provide pros and cons or side-by-side comparisons.

- **Translating technical language into plain English**: Perfect for non-coders learning new concepts.

Example 1: Comparing Frameworks

Prompt:

"Compare React and Vue.js for building a single-page application. Include pros and cons of each."

AI Summary:

- **React**:

  - Pros: Large community, reusable components, flexibility.

  - Cons: Requires additional tools (e.g., router, state management).

- **Vue**:

- Pros: Easy to learn, built-in features, great for beginners.

- Cons: Smaller ecosystem compared to React.

Checklist: AI Research for Frameworks

- Define your goal (e.g., build a single-page app).

- Ask AI to suggest tools or frameworks.

- Prompt AI for a comparison between top options.

- Ask for best practices related to the chosen tool.

Exercise 1:

Ask AI: "Summarize the Fetch API in JavaScript and give two examples of how to use it."

Learning New Tech with AI Guides

AI can serve as a customized teacher, giving you a structured, digestible learning plan tailored to your current level.

How to Ask AI for Learning Help:

- Ask AI to break down complex topics into beginner-friendly lessons.

- Request learning paths based on your goals.

- Use AI to create exercises, explain errors, and offer analogies.

Example 2: Learning Promises

Prompt:

> "Teach me JavaScript Promises like I'm a beginner. Include simple code examples and explain how they work."

AI Response (simplified):

```javascript
const myPromise = new Promise((resolve,
reject) => {
  setTimeout(() => {
    resolve("Done!");
  }, 1000);
});
myPromise.then(result => {
  console.log(result); // Outputs: Done!
});
```

Explanation: Promises represent future values. You can use `.then()` to do something when the promise is resolved.

Exercise 2:

Ask AI: "Explain JavaScript async/await with examples. Include a real-world analogy."

Staying Updated Without Drowning in Info Overload

The JavaScript ecosystem changes constantly — but you don't have to read every blog or scroll through hours of content. AI can help you stay informed without feeling overwhelmed.

Strategies for Staying Updated with AI:

- Ask AI to summarize the latest trends or updates.

- Request a bullet-point summary of major changes in new releases.

- Use AI to generate a learning plan based on what's relevant right now.

Example 3: Summarizing JavaScript Trends

Prompt:

> "Summarize the key trends in JavaScript for 2024. Focus on practical things beginners should know."

AI Response:

- Increased use of AI-powered tools (e.g., GitHub Copilot).

- Growing popularity of server-side rendering with tools like Next.js.

- Shift toward TypeScript for better code safety.

Action Item:

Set a weekly reminder to ask AI something like: "What are the most important JavaScript updates this month?"

Action Items for Practical Mastery:

- Use AI to create a customized weekly learning plan.

- Ask AI to summarize a new framework or library you're curious about.

- Practice explaining a new concept back to AI to reinforce your learning.

- Regularly check in with AI to see what's new — and what you should focus on next.

Multiple Choice Quiz (10 Questions)

Question 1: How can AI help when researching frameworks?
 A. Only recommend React
 B. Summarize and compare multiple options ✓
 C. Replace coding entirely
 D. Prevent you from learning
 Explanation: AI can summarize documentation and compare tools to help you make informed decisions.

Question 2: When using AI to learn new tech, you should:
 A. Ask for random facts
 B. Use it to create structured explanations and examples ✓
 C. Avoid asking for help
 D. Only use official docs
 Explanation: AI can teach you step-by-step with explanations tailored to your level.

Question 3: What is one way AI helps reduce info overload?
 A. By ignoring updates
 B. By summarizing complex topics and trends ✓
 C. By hiding resources
 D. By forcing you to read more
 Explanation: AI can distill large volumes of content into key takeaways.

Question 4: What's a good prompt for AI to help with research?
 A. "Tell me everything"
 B. "Explain React and Vue, and compare them." ✓
 C. "Make me a website"
 D. "Do my homework"
 Explanation: A clear comparison prompt helps AI deliver useful, targeted information.

Question 5: When learning something new, you can ask AI to:
 A. Explain using analogies ✓
 B. Avoid giving examples
 C. Test your math
 D. Write essays
 Explanation: Analogies help simplify technical concepts for beginners.

Question 6: What is a Promise in JavaScript?
 A. A debugging tool
 B. A future value ✓
 C. A static variable
 D. An event listener
 Explanation: A Promise represents a value that will be available later.

Question 7: To stay current, you should:
 A. Never ask AI questions
 B. Use AI to get summarized updates ✓
 C. Read every blog post
 D. Avoid learning new things
 Explanation: AI can provide curated and condensed information to help you keep up.

Question 8: How does AI help with best practices?

A. It ignores them

B. It creates custom guidelines and checklists ✓

C. It writes laws

D. It tests code in browsers

Explanation: AI can suggest best practices based on your specific context.

Question 9: A good use of AI for learning is:

A. Asking it to quiz you ✓

B. Asking it to play games

C. Asking it to paint

D. Avoiding all questions

Explanation: You can use AI to create quizzes and practice material for yourself.

Question 10: AI can create a personalized learning path by:

A. Guessing randomly

B. Asking about your goals and experience ✓

C. Avoiding questions

D. Following a static course

Explanation: AI can adjust content and structure based on your needs.

Chapter 10: Building More, Maintaining Less

As your JavaScript projects grow, they become more complex. You might worry about maintaining them, updating older code, or keeping everything running smoothly. The great news is that AI can help you scale your work without getting buried in manual upkeep. In this chapter, you'll learn how to use AI to scale codebases, upgrade legacy systems, and keep your projects healthy — so you can focus on building more and maintaining less.

Learning Objectives

By the end of this chapter, you will be able to:

- Use AI to help scale JavaScript codebases while reducing manual overhead.

- Apply AI to upgrade or migrate legacy JavaScript systems safely and efficiently.

- Maintain project health using AI-driven tools and automation for refactoring, linting, documentation, and testing.

- Practice sustainable coding with AI to reduce long-term technical debt.

Scaling Codebases Without Getting Buried

As your codebase grows, keeping it organized, readable, and efficient becomes more difficult. AI helps you manage this complexity by offering real-time suggestions, consistent refactoring, and even architectural guidance.

How AI Helps You Scale Codebases

- **Suggesting reusable components** to avoid duplicated code

- **Refactoring large files into smaller modules**

- **Detecting inconsistencies or code smells**

- **Maintaining consistent style and structure**

Real-World Example: Refactoring a Large File

Prompt to AI:

> "Refactor this large JavaScript file into reusable modules for better scalability."

Before:

```
function add(a, b) {
   return a + b;
}
function subtract(a, b) {
   return a - b;
}
function multiply(a, b) {
   return a * b;
}
function divide(a, b) {
   return a / b;
}
```

AI Suggestion: Separate each function into its own file or group similar operations in a `mathUtils.js` file.

```
// mathUtils.js
export function add(a, b) { return a + b; }
export function subtract(a, b) { return a -
b; }
export function multiply(a, b) { return a *
b; }
export function divide(a, b) { return a / b;
}
```

Checklist: Using AI to Scale Codebases

- Break large files into modules

- Ask AI for reusable component suggestions

- Use AI to check for duplicated code

- Request consistent refactoring patterns

Exercise 1:

Use AI to suggest how to refactor a long JavaScript file containing more than five functions into separate logical modules.

AI for Legacy System Upgrades and Migrations

Working with old JavaScript code (often called "legacy code") can be stressful. You might not know how it works, or it might be written using outdated syntax or libraries. AI can analyze, modernize, and explain legacy code, making it easier to bring up to modern standards.

How AI Can Help With Legacy Code:

- Translates old JavaScript syntax (ES5) into modern syntax (ES6+)

- Suggests migration paths for frameworks or libraries (e.g., jQuery → Vanilla JS or React)

- Explains confusing or undocumented code

Real-World Example: Modernizing Legacy Syntax

Legacy Code:

```
var name = "Alex";
function greet() {
  console.log("Hello " + name);
}
```

Prompt to AI:

> "Update this JavaScript code to use modern ES6+ syntax."

AI Response:

```
const name = "Alex";
const greet = () => {
  console.log(`Hello ${name}`);
};
```

Exercise 2:

Use AI to convert legacy jQuery code into modern Vanilla JavaScript or React components.

Keeping Projects Healthy with Less Manual Work

AI helps keep your project healthy and error-free by automating tedious maintenance tasks.

What AI Can Help Maintain Automatically:

- Linting and formatting code

- Identifying unused variables and functions

- Generating tests and documentation

- Refactoring repeated code blocks

- Suggesting performance improvements

Example: Automatic Linting and Formatting

Prompt:

> "Lint and format this code using standard JavaScript style."

Input Code:

```
function    sayHi(name){console.log("Hi
"+name);}
```

AI-Formatted Code:

```
function sayHi(name) {
  console.log(`Hi ${name}`);
}
```

Exercise 3:

Paste in a messy or inconsistent code block and ask AI to lint, format, and simplify it.

Action Items for Practical Mastery

- Refactor a cluttered JavaScript file using AI into multiple modules.

- Use AI to update an old script to modern syntax and best practices.

- Ask AI to generate automated tests or documentation for legacy functions.

- Regularly prompt AI to check for unused variables and recommend improvements.

Multiple Choice Quiz (10 Questions)

Question 1: What is one reason AI is useful when scaling a JavaScript codebase?
A. It writes entire applications instantly
B. It ensures consistent structure and reusable components ✓
C. It replaces developers
D. It avoids code testing
Explanation: AI can help maintain organization and consistency as your project grows.

Question 2: Legacy code refers to:
A. The most modern code
B. Deprecated or older codebases still in use ✓
C. Framework-specific code
D. Unreadable syntax
Explanation: Legacy code is often older or written using outdated practices or tools.

Question 3: What's a benefit of using AI for legacy upgrades?
  A. Makes the code more outdated
  B. Automatically writes untested code
  C. Suggests modern syntax and explains outdated parts ✓
  D. Deletes old code
Explanation: AI helps modernize syntax and bring clarity to legacy functions.

Question 4: What does AI-assisted linting do?
  A. Removes all comments
  B. Organizes and formats code according to style rules ✓
  C. Adds complexity
  D. Writes new frameworks
Explanation: Linting ensures your code is consistently written and readable.

Question 5: Why should you modularize your codebase?
  A. To make it harder to understand
  B. To improve scalability and readability ✓
  C. To reduce speed
  D. To avoid using imports
Explanation: Modular code is easier to manage, test, and maintain.

Question 6: Which AI prompt would best help refactor repetitive code?
  A. "Write random code."
  B. "Make this more confusing."
  C. "Identify and refactor repeated code blocks." ✓
  D. "Do nothing."
Explanation: AI can identify patterns and reduce redundancy when prompted properly.

Question 7: A benefit of using AI for maintenance is:
A. Constant manual updates
B. Less reliable code
C. Fewer repetitive tasks ✓
D. More copy-pasting
Explanation: AI automates routine checks, saving time and reducing errors.

Question 8: How can AI help migrate old JavaScript libraries?
A. Leave them as-is
B. Replace them silently
C. Suggest modern equivalents and update usage ✓
D. Delete them all
Explanation: AI can guide you to modern alternatives and help rewrite usage patterns.

Question 9: Which of the following tasks can AI assist with?
A. Writing new frameworks
B. Generating documentation for old code ✓
C. Avoiding code organization
D. Creating CSS-only apps
Explanation: AI is great at reading old code and writing summaries and usage guides.

Question 10: To keep a JavaScript project healthy, you should:
A. Ignore bugs
B. Rely solely on manual work
C. Use AI to automate repetitive checks and improvements ✓
D. Stop updating
Explanation: AI helps automate quality control so you can focus on building new features.

Chapter Conclusion

You did it! You now know how to scale your JavaScript projects confidently without getting stuck in maintenance mode. Whether you're refactoring large codebases, upgrading legacy systems, or maintaining a healthy workflow, AI is your trusted partner. By automating routine tasks and simplifying complexity, AI lets you build more while maintaining less — saving you time and reducing stress.

Now go take control of your codebase and let AI handle the heavy lifting.

Chapter 11: Collaborative Coding with AI

Working with AI isn't just about getting code written—it's about building smarter, more collaborative workflows. In this chapter, you'll learn how to work *with* AI like you would a teammate. Whether you're reviewing code, brainstorming new features, or trying to untangle a difficult problem, AI can be a powerful coding partner that improves both your speed and your confidence.

Learning Objectives

By the end of this chapter, you will be able to:

- Use AI to review your code and catch issues before human peer review.

- Collaborate with AI to brainstorm new features, designs, or improvements.

- Treat AI as a reliable "thinking partner" when solving difficult problems.

- Practice workflows where AI helps you build better, smarter, and cleaner JavaScript.

Using AI for Code Reviews (Before Peer Reviews)

Before you share your code with others, AI can help you polish it, catch bugs, and offer suggestions for improvement—just like a silent, ever-available reviewer.

What Can AI Help Review?

- Syntax errors and inconsistent formatting

- Unused variables or unreachable code

- Readability and clarity of function names and logic

- Suggestions for simplification or better practices

Example: Reviewing a Simple Function

Original Code:

```
function calc(x, y){
    return x*y;
}
```

Prompt:

> "Review this function. Suggest improvements or better practices."

AI Response:

- Rename the function to `multiply` for clarity.

- Add parameter validation.

- Include a comment explaining the function.

Improved Code:

```
// Multiplies two numbers and returns the
result
function multiply(x, y) {
```

```
  if (typeof x !== 'number' || typeof y !==
'number') {
    throw new Error("Both arguments must be
numbers.");
  }
  return x * y;
}
```

Checklist: Pre-Peer Code Review with AI

- Prompt AI to review function clarity and purpose

- Ask for suggestions on naming, readability, and best practices

- Request AI to identify unused or inefficient code

- Apply AI feedback before sharing with a human reviewer

Exercise 1:

Write a function that checks if a string is a palindrome. Then, prompt AI to review it for readability and best practices.

Brainstorming New Features and Architectures with AI

AI isn't just for fixing problems—it can help you *invent*. You can use it to brainstorm new features, improve existing ones, or even explore alternative ways to build your app.

How to Collaborate with AI During Brainstorming

- Share your project goals or current features

- Ask "what if" questions to explore new possibilities

- Use follow-up prompts to refine vague ideas into code-ready specs

Example: Feature Brainstorming

Prompt:

> "I'm building a to-do list app. What are five features I could add to make it more useful?"

AI Response:

1. Tagging or categorizing tasks

2. Due date reminders

3. Priority levels (high, medium, low)

4. Task completion analytics

5. Drag-and-drop task reordering

Exercise 2:

Tell AI about your current or imaginary project and ask for 3–5 additional features that would improve the user experience.

AI as a Thought Partner for Tough Problems

You might get stuck trying to figure out *how* to solve a problem. In those moments, AI is like a rubber duck that talks back. It can help you explore logic, troubleshoot bugs, or compare different solutions.

Problem-Solving Prompts:

- "Why isn't this working the way I expect?"

- "Can you explain what this code does line by line?"

- "Is there a better way to solve this problem?"

- "Help me break this big task into smaller steps."

Example: Debugging a Logic Issue

Problem:

```
function isEven(num) {
   return num % 2;
}
```

Prompt to AI:

"This function isn't working right. Can you explain why?"

AI Explanation: The function returns 0 for even numbers and 1 for odd numbers. Use `return num % 2 === 0` instead for a `true/false` response.

Corrected Code:

```
function isEven(num) {
   return num % 2 === 0;
}
```

Exercise 3:

Try writing a function to calculate a user's age based on their birth year. Use AI to help you break it into smaller tasks, write the function, and then review it together.

Action Items for Practical Mastery

- Practice asking AI to review every new function you write before peer review.

- Start brainstorming new features or interface ideas with AI during planning stages.

- Use AI when you get stuck — treat it like a senior developer who helps guide your thinking.

- Create a list of your top 3 AI prompts for reviewing, brainstorming, and debugging.

Multiple Choice Quiz (10 Questions)

Question 1: What's the benefit of reviewing code with AI before human review?
 A. It prevents collaboration
 B. It ensures your code is perfect
 C. It helps catch small issues and polish code ✓
 D. It writes new features automatically
 Explanation: AI can offer helpful suggestions so your code is cleaner before others see it.

Question 2: Which of these is a valid use of AI in brainstorming?
 A. Writing bad code
 B. Suggesting new features or improvements ✅
 C. Avoiding user feedback
 D. Disabling your editor
 Explanation: AI is great for generating and refining ideas for new features.

Question 3: How can AI act as a thought partner?
 A. By solving all problems instantly
 B. By rubber-ducking your questions and offering guidance ✅
 C. By rewriting your project
 D. By replacing all team members
 Explanation: You can talk through your thought process with AI to get insight.

Question 4: What's a good prompt to use when stuck on a bug?
 A. "Fix this now."
 B. "This is broken."
 C. "Why isn't this working the way I expect?" ✅
 D. "Delete everything."
 Explanation: Explaining your expectations helps AI troubleshoot the issue.

Question 5: What's a key feature of AI-based code review?
 A. Rewrites everything
 B. Only tests the UI
 C. Suggests improvements and detects bad practices ✅
 D. Ignores syntax
 Explanation: AI code reviews can catch inefficiencies and offer improvements.

Question 6: A brainstorming session with AI might include:
 A. Asking about vacation spots
 B. Rewriting HTML only
 C. Exploring alternative architectural designs ✅
 D. Skipping design decisions
 Explanation: AI can help you evaluate different ways to structure your application.

Question 7: When should you ask AI to review your function?
 A. After the final release
 B. Before you ask a teammate for feedback ✅
 C. After deleting it
 D. Only when you have an error
 Explanation: AI can help you polish your code before others review it.

Question 8: What does the prompt "Help me break this into smaller parts" do?
 A. It writes a database
 B. Helps decompose large problems into manageable steps ✅
 C. Changes code randomly
 D. Deletes your code
 Explanation: This helps you break complex logic into actionable pieces.

Question 9: One benefit of AI feedback is:
 A. It always disagrees with you
 B. It makes you code faster and cleaner ✅
 C. It replaces comments
 D. It runs your code
 Explanation: AI feedback helps you improve the clarity and efficiency of your code.

Question 10: When you brainstorm with AI, what should you provide?
 A. A vague sentence
 B. A description of your project or goal ✓
 C. A bug report
 D. A screenshot
 Explanation: Clear context helps AI suggest useful features or improvements.

Chapter Conclusion

You're not coding alone anymore. In this chapter, you learned how to collaborate with AI like a teammate — to review code, brainstorm ideas, and work through tough problems together. With this approach, your code will be clearer, your thinking will be sharper, and your project will move faster. Keep practicing this habit of collaborative coding, and you'll never get stuck for long. Let AI help you think, grow, and build with confidence.

Chapter 12: Increasing Creativity, Not Just Speed

AI is often praised for making work faster—but it can also make you more creative. In this chapter, we'll explore how AI can help you think more freely, experiment with ideas, and refine your coding craft. Whether you're designing a user interface, building a new feature, or improving your code's elegance, AI is not just your accelerator—it's your creative amplifier.

Learning Objectives

By the end of this chapter, you will be able to:

- Understand how AI can unlock creative thinking in JavaScript development.

- Balance fast prototyping with high-quality, maintainable code.

- Use AI to amplify your unique coding style, strengths, and design ideas.

- Build interactive features or solutions that go beyond the basics.

- Practice generating original solutions with AI as a collaborative partner.

How AI Frees You to Be More Creative

When you're not bogged down by boilerplate code, repetitive tasks, or syntax frustrations, your mind has space to think about what's possible — not just what's required. AI can handle the routine parts of coding so you can focus on:

- Creating visually engaging user experiences

- Experimenting with new interactions or logic

- Refining features based on user needs

- Exploring multiple ways to solve a problem

Real-World Example: Creative Input Field

Prompt:

> "Create a JavaScript input field that gives instant emoji feedback based on the sentiment of the typed message."

AI Output:

```
const input =
document.querySelector('#message');
const emoji =
document.querySelector('#emoji');
input.addEventListener('input', () => {
  const value = input.value.toLowerCase();
  if (value.includes('happy')) {
    emoji.textContent = '☺';
  } else if (value.includes('angry')) {
    emoji.textContent = '😖';
  } else if (value.includes('love')) {
    emoji.textContent = '♥ ';
  } else {
    emoji.textContent = ' ';
```

```
    }
});
```

This simple idea creates a delightful experience. Without AI, the technical barriers might prevent you from even trying it.

Exercise 1:

Ask AI to help you create a "mood button" that changes color based on keywords typed by the user (e.g., "excited" = orange, "calm" = blue).

Balancing Speed with Craftsmanship

AI helps you code faster, but the goal isn't just speed — it's quality. Creative coding means thinking about:

- Code that's clear, reusable, and beautiful

- Experiences that are meaningful to users

- Building with empathy and purpose

How to Balance Speed and Craft:

Fast with AI	Balanced with Craftsmanship
Quickly generate layout with AI	Refine layout for accessibility
Auto-generate function logic	Add meaningful comments and naming
Build a prototype in minutes	Polish with animations, UX details

Prompt Examples for Craftsmanship:

- "Can you make this form more user-friendly and accessible?"

- "Add transitions to improve the user experience."

- "Refactor this logic to make it easier to understand."

Exercise 2:

Write a basic to-do app with AI, then refine it by:

- Adding smooth fade-in animations for tasks

- Improving error handling

- Giving each feature a clear label and helpful comments

AI as an Amplifier of Your Best Skills

AI doesn't replace your creativity — it enhances it. You bring the ideas, instincts, and imagination. AI brings the speed, structure, and suggestions.

How to Amplify Your Strengths with AI:

If you're a visual thinker:
Prompt AI to help you build dynamic UIs and animations.

If you love logic puzzles:
Ask AI to generate alternative algorithms and help you compare them.

If you're detail-oriented:
Use AI to review and refine your code's clarity, performance, and style.

Example: Using AI to Compare Solutions

Prompt:

> "What are two different ways to filter an array of numbers to get only the even ones in JavaScript?"

AI Response:

```
// Option 1: Using filter
const evenNumbers = numbers.filter(num =>
num % 2 === 0);
// Option 2: Using a for loop
const evenNumbers = [];
for (let num of numbers) {
  if (num % 2 === 0) {
    evenNumbers.push(num);
  }
}
```

You get to pick which one suits your style or performance needs best.

Checklist: Becoming a Creative Coder with AI

- Use AI to generate starting points for your ideas

- Experiment with multiple solutions to the same problem

- Use follow-up prompts to refine AI-generated code

- Add your own personal style and improvements

Action Items for Practical Mastery

- Create a fun mini project (like a color picker or animated timer) with AI assistance.

- Use AI to suggest three versions of the same feature, and choose the one you like best.

- Prompt AI to improve the UX or creativity of one of your recent code snippets.

- Ask AI to rephrase code in your voice: "Make this code more fun and expressive."

Multiple Choice Quiz (10 Questions)

Question 1: What is one way AI increases creativity in coding?
A. It locks you into one way of thinking
B. It removes all style from your code
C. It handles repetitive tasks so you can focus on ideas ✅
D. It avoids asking questions
Explanation: AI frees your mental energy for creative design and feature building.

Question 2: A key difference between speed and craftsmanship is:
A. Speed always produces better code
B. Craftsmanship includes clarity, user experience, and care ✅
C. Craftsmanship is only for experts
D. Speed skips syntax
Explanation: Craftsmanship involves thoughtful refinement beyond functionality.

Question 3: How can AI help visual learners in JavaScript?
A. By reading books
B. By generating UI examples and animations ✓
C. By writing documentation only
D. By showing SQL
Explanation: AI can produce interactive UI code that helps visual thinkers explore ideas.

Question 4: AI is most effective creatively when:
A. You follow every suggestion blindly
B. You ask open-ended and playful prompts ✓
C. You use it only for math
D. You copy and paste code without reading it
Explanation: The best creativity comes from guiding AI with thoughtful prompts.

Question 5: Which is an example of balancing speed with craft?
A. Writing code fast and not testing
B. Auto-generating layout and adding custom animations ✓
C. Skipping comments to save time
D. Avoiding accessibility
Explanation: Balancing speed with polish improves both user and developer experience.

Question 6: What type of prompt amplifies creativity?
A. "Fix this bug."
B. "Generate three ways to build this feature." ✓
C. "Write fast."
D. "Use the default method."
Explanation: Asking for multiple options sparks comparison and decision-making.

Question 7: What does it mean to be a creative coder?

A. Only write new code

B. Use AI to create confusing projects

C. Mix logic with design, empathy, and experimentation ✓

D. Avoid using tools

Explanation: Creative coders use code to solve problems in thoughtful, user-focused ways.

Question 8: When AI writes a function, how should you respond?

A. Trust it completely

B. Read, test, and refine it ✓

C. Assume it's incorrect

D. Translate it to another language

Explanation: Reviewing and improving AI output makes you a better coder.

Question 9: If you're stuck creatively, what should you do?

A. Give up

B. Ask AI for feature suggestions or alternatives ✓

C. Keep rewriting the same code

D. Avoid making decisions

Explanation: AI can suggest fresh directions and help you brainstorm new ideas.

Question 10: Which activity best supports AI-assisted creativity?

A. Memorizing syntax

B. Prompting AI for colorful and fun UI ideas ✓

C. Copying outdated code

D. Using only default settings

Explanation: Creative prompts allow AI to offer more unique, engaging solutions.

Chapter Conclusion

AI doesn't just make you faster—it makes you freer. In this chapter, you learned how AI unlocks your creative potential, helps you craft more thoughtful solutions, and supports you in building work that's both functional and delightful. With the right mindset and prompts, AI becomes your creative sidekick, helping you build better, brighter, and more personalized JavaScript projects.

Bonus Section: Templates and Cheat Sheets

This bonus section is your go-to guide for working faster and smarter with AI in your JavaScript projects. Whether you're coding, debugging, exploring new ideas, or just trying to stay productive, the following templates, reference materials, and tools will help you streamline your process and reduce guesswork.

Learning Objectives

By the end of this section, you will:

- Be able to use prompt templates to consistently get quality JavaScript code from AI.

- Quickly diagnose and fix issues using AI-powered debugging strategies.

- Choose the right AI tools for different tasks with confidence.

- Apply dozens of productivity-boosting techniques that combine JavaScript and AI.

Best Prompt Templates for JavaScript Development

Writing clear prompts is half the battle when working with AI. These templates help you get accurate, readable, and useful JavaScript code from AI tools.

General Purpose Coding Prompts

- "Write a JavaScript function that [does something specific]. Provide at least one example."
  Example:
  "Write a JavaScript function that checks if a number is prime. Provide an example."

- "Explain what this JavaScript function does, and suggest improvements for readability."
  Use this when reviewing existing code.

- "Refactor the following JavaScript code to make it more efficient and easier to read."

- "Convert this function to use ES6 arrow function syntax and template literals."

UI/DOM-Related Prompts

- "Create a JavaScript function that updates the content of a `<div>` when a button is clicked."

- "Write code to validate an HTML form using JavaScript and show custom error messages."

- "Add a fade-in animation using JavaScript when an element is added to the page."

API and Data Handling Prompts

- "Write a JavaScript function that fetches data from [API URL] and logs the result."

- "Use async/await to handle API responses and show an error message if the call fails."

- "Create a function that displays data in a table format using the response from an API."

Exercise: Create Your Own Prompt Template

Write down a common coding task you do often. Now craft a reusable AI prompt that you can apply to similar problems in the future. Save it in a document for later use.

Quick Reference for AI Debugging Techniques

When something goes wrong in your JavaScript code, AI can help you debug more quickly — if you know how to ask.

Debugging Checklist Using AI

- **Copy the exact error message** and include it in your prompt.

- **Paste the code snippet** that's causing the issue.

- **Explain the expected behavior vs. the actual result.**

- **Ask AI to suggest reasons for the problem** and possible solutions.

Prompt Templates for Debugging

- "Why is this JavaScript code throwing an error: [insert code + error message]?"

- "This code is returning **undefined**. Can you help me understand why?"

- "My loop runs forever. What's wrong with this while loop: [insert loop code]?"

- "Refactor this function to avoid duplication and improve performance."

- "Explain what this error means and how I can fix it: Uncaught TypeError: Cannot read property 'x' of undefined."

Exercise: Practice Debugging Prompt

Take a small function that you know has a bug. Prompt AI using the checklist above. Reflect on what kind of response you receive and how accurate it is.

AI Tools Comparison Chart

There are many tools that help you write JavaScript with AI. Here's a quick reference comparing some of the most popular ones based on common use cases.

Tool	Best For	Strengths	Limitations
ChatGPT	Conversational help and code explanation	Excellent at explaining code and fixing bugs	Not integrated into your editor
GitHub Copilot	Real-time code suggestions in your editor	Autocompletes code, recognizes context	Limited natural language interaction

Codeium	Fast code generation and autocomplete	Lightweight, fast, supports many languages	May need refinement for clarity
Claude (Anthropic)	Writing and reviewing complex functions	Offers structured output and clean formatting	Not optimized for step-by-step debugging
Bard / Gemini	Simple solutions and concept summaries	Good for learning high-level concepts quickly	Not great for detailed coding sessions

30 Quick Productivity Hacks with AI

Use these small but powerful ideas to get more done with less effort.

Code Generation Hacks

1. Prompt AI to generate boilerplate for projects (HTML, CSS, JS).

2. Ask for alternate implementations to compare speed/readability.

3. Use AI to comment or document old code you didn't write.

4. Translate jQuery code into modern JavaScript.

5. Get example usages for any JavaScript method (e.g., `.map()`, `.reduce()`).

Debugging Hacks

6. Paste error messages and ask for likely causes.

7. Use AI to isolate logic in small testable functions.

8. Ask AI to suggest test cases for your function.

9. Let AI write basic unit tests with Jest or Mocha.

10. Ask "What could cause this error in JavaScript?" for broad issues.

Learning & Research Hacks

11. Ask AI to explain concepts like Promises, closures, or hoisting in plain English.

12. Create a glossary of JavaScript terms using AI.

13. Get a curated list of JavaScript tutorials on a topic you're learning.

14. Ask for a learning path based on your goals.

15. Let AI quiz you on key terms you want to memorize.

Code Style & Quality Hacks

16. Ask AI to lint and format your code according to a style guide.

17. Request performance tips for a specific function.

18. Use AI to identify duplicated logic or patterns.

19. Get suggestions for more readable variable or function names.

20. Ask AI to rewrite code for better modularity.

Brainstorming Hacks

21. Prompt AI to generate 10 fun ideas for projects.

22. Use AI to design a simple game mechanic.

23. Ask for interactive UI element suggestions.

24. Collaborate with AI to plan app features and structure.

25. Ask for 3 variations of the same feature with pros and cons.

Miscellaneous Productivity Boosters

26. Build a JavaScript cheat sheet from AI responses.

27. Use AI to summarize documentation pages.

28. Create reusable code snippet libraries from AI output.

29. Ask AI to write social posts or descriptions about your project.

30. Create custom AI prompt templates for specific workflows.

Final Action Items

- Create a personal Google Doc or Notion page with your favorite prompt templates.

- Start building a reusable AI-powered "cheat sheet" folder for common functions.

- Practice debugging with AI by reviewing one old project and applying suggestions.

- Choose one AI tool and use it daily for a week to become fluent in its capabilities.

- Reflect on how AI has shifted your workflow — and how you can lean on it more creatively.

By using these templates, techniques, and hacks, you're not just learning to code — you're learning to *code with power*. AI helps you speed up, but more importantly, it helps you code with more confidence, clarity, and creativity.

Final Thoughts

As we reach the end of this journey, it's important to pause and reflect on where we've been — and where we're going. You've learned how to use AI to write JavaScript, troubleshoot errors, build creative features, and level up your coding workflow. But this is only the beginning. JavaScript is still evolving, and AI is becoming a more integrated part of how we build, learn, and collaborate in the tech world.

This chapter isn't about teaching a new tool or coding trick. Instead, it's about preparing you for the future of development: a future where AI and human developers work side by side to build amazing things. By the end of this chapter, you'll understand how to keep growing as a developer, how to use AI thoughtfully, and why your creativity, judgment, and vision matter more than ever.

Learning Objectives

By the end of this chapter, you will:

- Understand the emerging trends in AI-powered JavaScript development.

- Learn how to grow your skills and stay relevant in a rapidly changing environment.

- Recognize the irreplaceable qualities human developers bring to the table.

- Feel empowered to create, experiment, and lead in the age of AI.

The Future of JavaScript Development with AI

AI isn't replacing developers—it's redefining what developers can do. In the coming years, AI will continue to handle more of the repetitive, mechanical work, while humans will guide the direction, purpose, and quality of what's being built.

Here's what the future might look like:

1. Faster and Smarter Workflows

- AI will integrate more deeply into code editors and cloud tools.

- Developers will rely on natural language more than syntax to express intent.

- Code generation will become more collaborative and conversational.

2. More Accessible Learning Paths

- Beginners can jump into JavaScript with help from AI tutors.

- No-code and low-code platforms will merge with AI-driven scripting.

3. Human-Centered Development

- Developers will focus more on user needs, design thinking, and problem-solving.

- Creativity and empathy will be critical in deciding how features are built.

Real-World Example: Future Workflow

145

Let's imagine you're asked to build a budgeting app:

- You describe the user experience in plain English: *"I want users to add income and expenses and see a live chart."*

- AI helps scaffold the layout and data logic.

- You review, refine, and adjust the code based on your own design preferences.

- You add thoughtful touches: accessibility features, tooltips, and branding.

The AI wrote the base. You made it meaningful.

How to Stay Ahead (and Stay Human)

You don't need to race against AI. Instead, grow alongside it.

Checklist: Staying Ahead in the Age of AI

- **Keep practicing core JavaScript skills.** The fundamentals still matter.

- **Use AI to learn, not just to finish.** Ask *why*, not just *how*.

- **Explore creative coding projects.** Try animations, games, art, or tools.

- **Engage with the community.** Ask questions, share ideas, teach others.

- **Stay curious.** Don't rely on what you know — keep exploring what you don't.

Action Items:

- Create a "learning habit." Choose one small JavaScript or AI concept to explore each week.

- Follow at least one blog, podcast, or newsletter that covers AI and web development.

- Write a short reflection after building something with AI: *What did I learn? What could I improve next time?*

The Developer's Role in the Age of AI: Creativity, Judgment, and Vision

No matter how good AI becomes, it still lacks three critical things you bring to the table:

1. Creativity

You dream up features no one asked for. You see connections between ideas. You imagine what could exist, not just what already does.

AI can generate. But only you can innovate.

2. Judgment

You make choices. You consider ethical concerns, edge cases, accessibility, and human needs. AI doesn't know what's "good" — you do.

Your code reflects your values. Your decisions shape the experience.

3. Vision

You think about the big picture. What should this app do? How should it feel? Who is it for? What problem does it solve?

AI can suggest tools. You create tools that matter.

Challenge: Define Your Developer Identity

Take 10 minutes to reflect on this:

- What kinds of problems do I enjoy solving?

- What values do I want to bring to my projects?

- How do I want to grow as a developer in the next year?

- How can I use AI to support that growth?

Write it down. This is your personal developer mission.

Final Action Plan

- Use AI not just to build faster, but to **think bigger**.

- Balance technical ability with **creative exploration**.

- Develop your own voice and values as a developer.

- Stay engaged, stay humble, and **stay human**.

As you move forward, remember: AI is your partner. It's not here to replace you — it's here to **amplify you**. Every line of code you write with AI is still yours. Every idea you refine through conversation, every app you build through collaboration — that's your work, powered by possibility.

Conclusion: Your Journey Is Just Beginning

Congratulations! You've made it through the book—and that's no small achievement. Whether you're brand new to coding or returning with a fresh perspective, you've now seen how AI can revolutionize your approach to JavaScript. But more importantly, you've developed something even more valuable: the mindset of a modern, empowered developer.

You've learned how to:

- Prompt AI to help you write, explain, debug, and refactor JavaScript code.

- Accelerate your learning and development by collaborating with intelligent tools.

- Build working projects faster through rapid prototyping and clear architectural planning.

- Write cleaner, smarter code with the help of unit tests, mock data, and debugging playbooks.

This is just the beginning. With every line of code you write and every project you create, you'll deepen your skills and confidence. AI is your coding partner—but **you** are the driver. You bring the creativity, the goals, the questions, and the vision. AI helps you execute, explore, and improve faster than ever before.

As you continue your journey:

- Keep experimenting. There's no better way to learn than by doing.

- Keep prompting. The more clearly you communicate with AI, the better your outcomes.

- Keep refining. Every piece of feedback, test result, and refactor helps you grow.

Your future as a developer is no longer limited by long, frustrating learning curves. Now, you have tools that adapt to your needs, support your goals, and give you the freedom to build with confidence — even if you don't know "everything" yet.

And that's the real superpower: **You know how to learn, how to build, and how to grow — with AI by your side.**

About the Author: Laurence Svekis

Laurence Svekis is an award-winning developer, educator, and author with over two decades of experience teaching web development and automation. With more than a million students worldwide, Laurence is best known for his approachable teaching style, clear explanations, and ability to simplify even the most complex programming topics.

A recognized Google Developer Expert (GDE) for Google Workspace and a leading voice in the tech education community, Laurence has created hundreds of tutorials, courses, and books on JavaScript, Google Apps Script, Python, and front-end web development. He's passionate about helping learners of all levels unlock their creative potential through code — especially when paired with the power of AI.

Through live presentations, university-level instruction, and hands-on workshops, Laurence empowers non-coders and seasoned developers alike to write better code, faster. His mission is simple: **make technology accessible, enjoyable, and transformative for everyone.**

Learn more about Laurence's latest projects, books, and resources at BaseScripts.com.

www.ingramcontent.com/pod-product-compliance
Lightning Source LLC
LaVergne TN
LVHW051242050326
832903LV00028B/2526